POP BUCHANAN

# Invest AI Robotics: The Quantum and Crypto Frontier

*How Artificial Intelligence, Quantum Computing, Robotics, and Blockchain Will Shape the Next 40 Years of Stock Investments, DePIN Systems, and Human Evolution*

*Financial and Educational Disclaimer*

*The information in this book is for educational, motivational, and entertainment purposes only. It is not financial advice, investment guidance, or a recommendation to buy, sell, or trade any security, asset, token, or investment product.*

*I am not a licensed financial adviser, stockbroker, investment analyst, or accredited investor. I do not manage money for others, and I do not offer individualized or professional financial advice. Nothing in this book should be interpreted as legal, tax, financial, or investment advice.*

*The ideas, theories, and examples shared in this book are based on open-source research, public market data, and educational study. They are intended to inspire critical thinking and help readers understand trends in technology, innovation, and business. Readers should always perform their own due diligence before making any financial or investment decision.*

*All market information, forecasts, and examples are for illustration and general discussion. Past performance does not guarantee future results. Markets can rise and fall quickly, and all forms of investing carry risk, including the loss of principal.*

*Readers should consult a qualified professional such as a licensed financial adviser, certified public accountant, or attorney before making decisions involving money, investments, or business ventures.*

*This book is not sponsored by, affiliated with, or endorsed by any of the companies, funds, or projects mentioned. References to specific organizations, products, or digital assets are for educational context only.*

*By reading this book, you agree that the author, publisher, and associated parties are not responsible for any financial loss, investment outcome, or decision made based on the material provided. The purpose of this book is to educate, motivate, and encourage curiosity about the future of technology and innovation, not to provide investment instruction.*

*Always research deeply, think independently, and invest only what you can afford to lose.*

*First edition*

*This book was professionally typeset on Reedsy.*
*Find out more at reedsy.com*

# Contents

# Introduction

## The Road from Algorithms to Organoids

*Every great change in technology begins with an idea that once seemed impossible. Then one day it becomes real.*

When I wrote Invest AI, my goal was to help people see that artificial intelligence was not magic. It was a new kind of market. I wanted readers to understand that data is money, and algorithms are the new machines of the modern world. That book showed how companies like Google, Amazon, and Microsoft used AI to build powerful industries around learning, prediction, and automation.

Then I wrote Invest AI Quantum. That book explored the next level of computing, one built on the strange and beautiful laws of quantum physics. It explained how qubits and superposition are not science fiction, but real tools used by companies such as IBM and D-Wave to solve problems too complex for normal computers. Quantum computing opened a door to a world where machines can explore millions of possibilities at once.

Now we arrive at the third book in the trilogy, Invest AI Robotics. This is where intelligence comes to life. Robots are no longer just arms in factories or props in movies. They are real, working beside us and learning as they move. They deliver packages, build cars, assist doctors, and explore space. Companies like Boston Dynamics, Figure AI, and Agility Robotics are creating machines that improve with every experience.

For investors, this is not just another phase of automation. It is a new kind of industry, one where movement, learning, and physical intelligence are valuable resources. We are no longer teaching machines only to think. We are teaching them to act.

Artificial intelligence gave us the digital brain. Quantum computing gave us the deep mind that can see endless patterns. Robotics gives us the body. Together they form a new kind of life made of metal, code, and motion. Every movement now carries millions of hidden calculations.

This book explores that world. It is about the rise of intelligent matter. It shows how machines are beginning to think through physical form.

The robotics market is growing quickly. By 2030, it could reach almost 200 billion dollars. Robots are working in factories, hospitals, warehouses, and homes. They are faster, cheaper, and safer than ever before. The parts that make this possible, such as sensors, chips, batteries, and software, hold the real value. Companies like NVIDIA, Siemens, ABB, Rockwell, and AMD are building the systems that connect intelligence with motion.

This book also looks at what comes next. It explores what happens when machines start to merge with biology and learn from living systems. Scientists at Johns Hopkins, Harvard, and MIT are growing brain-like tissue to power learning systems. These organoids may one day guide robots, power computers, and transform medicine. It sounds like science fiction, but it is already happening inside real laboratories.

That is why this book is called The Road from Algorithms to Organoids. It tells the story of how ideas become machines, and how machines may soon grow into living systems.

Reading this book will not make you a scientist, but it will make you a better observer. You will begin to see patterns in the news, the markets, and the world around you. You will learn how technology, investment, and creativity come together to shape the future.

My goal is not to predict stock prices. It is to help you understand momentum, the energy that moves new ideas from laboratories into markets. The companies that master this energy are the ones that define each new era.

We are now standing at the edge of the next one. Robots will become more human. Computers will become more alive. Biology will become programmable.

This is the story of how intelligence becomes real. It is the story of the future of work, energy, and life itself.

*Invest AI* showed us how machines learned to think.
*Invest AI Quantum* showed us how they learned to imagine.
Now *Invest AI Robotics* shows us how they learn to move.

Welcome to the age of intelligent matter, where life, learning, and technology finally meet.

# 1

# The Shift from Digital to Physical AI

Artificial intelligence began as thought without form. Early AI lived inside computers, sorting images, predicting markets, and learning language. It changed the digital world but did not yet move through the physical one. That transformation is happening now.

Today, robots think with the same neural networks that once powered search engines. They weld steel, deliver groceries, and assist in surgery. Intelligence has moved from the cloud into motion.

Analysts estimate that industries using AI-driven robotics gain between thirty and fifty percent more productivity within five years (McKinsey & Company, 2024). The global robotics market is projected to reach about 185 billion U.S. dollars by 2030 (Mordor Intelligence, 2025). These figures mark a turning point where automation becomes a foundation of daily life rather than a distant idea.

For investors, this signals new patterns of value. During the first AI wave, software and data made winners of companies such as NVIDIA and Microsoft. In the robotics era, value spreads through the supply chain, including hardware, sensors, batteries, and control systems. Firms such as ABB, Siemens, and Rockwell Automation now merge industrial equipment with embedded intelligence. Emerging humanoid builders such as Figure AI and Agility Robotics are experimenting with machines that can walk, lift, and learn (McKinsey & Company, 2024).

The line between software and hardware is fading. A robot has become a physical computer that learns by interacting with reality.

Invest AI Viewpoint
Our research indicates that the next surge of growth will come from machines that act, not only predict. Embodied intelligence, the union of AI, quantum optimization, and robotic motion, will define the 2030s in the same way social media defined the 2010s.

Investor Takeaways
Study public companies integrating AI into automation, including ABB (ABBN.SW), Siemens (SIE.DE), and Rockwell Automation (ROK). Watch private humanoid startups such as Figure AI, Sanctuary AI, and Apptronik that may later enter public markets. Track suppliers of servo motors, sensors, and control chips that power every autonomous system. Explore diversified AI and robotics exchange-traded funds such as ROBO and BOTZ for broad exposure.

# 2

# From GPUs to Robot Hands

Every robot begins as math. The same graphical processors that once helped video games render light and motion now help machines see, plan, and act. Graphics processing units, or GPUs, gave artificial intelligence the power to learn from images and text. Today, those same chips drive mechanical movement.

**The Hardware Revolution**

In the early 2000s, CPUs processed simple instructions one step at a time. GPUs could perform thousands simultaneously. When researchers trained neural networks on GPUs, learning times dropped from months to days (NVIDIA, 2023). That acceleration turned computer vision, speech recognition, and large language models into real industries.

Now, the same hardware logic fuels physical systems. Robotics platforms use GPUs and specialized AI accelerators to run control algorithms in real time. An industrial arm can adjust torque in microseconds because its embedded processor reads sensor feedback and predicts motion before it happens.

The hardware stack has expanded. Central processors still handle planning. GPUs and tensor chips manage perception and decision. Servo drives, actuators, and embedded controllers translate those calculations into motion. This layered approach allows an autonomous drone to fly or a humanoid robot to walk without falling.

**Building the Body of Intelligence**

Hardware suppliers quietly shape every leap in robotics.

Semiconductors: NVIDIA (NVDA), AMD (AMD), and Intel (INTC) supply the neural processing cores.
Control and Automation: ABB (ABBN.SW), Siemens (SIE.DE), and Rockwell Automation (ROK) integrate compute with factory systems.
Precision Motion: FANUC (6954.T), Yaskawa Electric (6506.T), and Harmonic Drive (6324.T) provide the motors, gears, and encoders that make motion smooth.
Sensors and Vision: Cognex (CGNX), Keyence (6861.T), and Basler (BAS.DE) give robots sight.

Together, these layers form the physical infrastructure of artificial intelligence.

**The Quantum Boost**

Quantum computing will not replace GPUs soon, but it already influences how robotics optimize tasks. Early studies show that quantum algorithms can improve path planning and materials design for lighter, stronger actuators (IBM Research, 2024). As hybrid quantum-classical systems mature, robotic simulations will train faster and with higher accuracy.

**Energy and Heat**

All computing produces heat, and robotics runs continuously. Energy-efficient chips are now a competitive advantage. Edge processors from companies such as Qualcomm (QCOM) and STMicroelectronics (STM) reduce latency and power draw. This trend connects sustainability with profitability, making green compute another investment theme.

**Invest AI Viewpoint**

Hardware is destiny. Every leap in artificial intelligence begins when new chips make new behavior possible. The next decade of robotics depends on semiconductors that merge high-speed computation with low-power efficiency. As production scales, the same chips that teach robots to move will appear in vehicles, appliances, and personal devices. Investors who understand this hardware migration will see opportunity long before mainstream funds do.

**Investor Takeaways**

Watch semiconductor leaders (NVIDIA, AMD, Intel) and edge-chip innovators (Qualcomm, STMicroelectronics). Study automation integrators (ABB, Siemens, Rockwell Automation) and motion-control specialists (FANUC, Yaskawa, Harmonic Drive). Follow sensor and vision suppliers (Cognex, Keyence, Basler) whose technology defines robotic perception.
Track developments in quantum-assisted simulation from IBM and Rigetti for long-term exposure.

Evaluate ETFs and funds with balanced hardware and automation portfolios.

# 3

# Quantum Acceleration

Artificial intelligence learns by pattern. Quantum computing learns by probability. When the two combine, discovery speeds up. Quantum acceleration means using quantum principles to improve how machines calculate, design, and move.

What Quantum Computing Does

Traditional computers store data as bits, zeros and ones. Quantum computers use qubits that can exist as both zero and one at the same time through a property called superposition. Qubits can also become entangled, meaning the state of one affects the other even at a distance. This allows some calculations to occur in parallel instead of sequentially.

For robotics and machine learning, this change matters because optimization problems are everywhere. A robot plans the shortest path to move an arm, balance on one foot, or deliver a package through traffic. Quantum algorithms can explore many routes at once, reducing energy use and decision time (IBM Research, 2024).

From Simulation to Design

Quantum computing is already transforming materials science and chemistry. Startups and research labs use it to design lighter alloys, longer-lasting batteries, and superconducting sensors (Rigetti Computing, 2024). Each breakthrough feeds directly into robotics. Stronger materials mean lighter frames. Better batteries extend run time. Improved sensors enhance balance and precision.

Companies such as D-Wave focus on quantum annealing, a method that finds the best solutions among millions of possibilities. This technique has shown promise in logistics scheduling and supply chain management (D-Wave Systems, 2023). Google Quantum AI and IonQ test similar algorithms for machine learning tasks. These advances suggest a future where quantum simulations train robots faster than real-world testing.

The Early Market

Quantum computing remains young but investable.
Public players include IBM (IBM), D-Wave Quantum Inc. (QBTS), IonQ (IONQ), and Rigetti (RGTI), all listed on major exchanges. Private innovators such as Xanadu in Canada and PsiQuantum in the United States pursue photonic approaches that may prove more scalable. Allied sectors include cloud computing firms such as Amazon and Microsoft, which rent early quantum access through their platforms. Most analysts agree that commercial quantum applications are five to ten years from mass deployment (McKinsey & Company, 2024). Yet, as GPUs did in 2010, the groundwork laid now can create enormous leverage later.

Hybrid Intelligence

The near future is hybrid. Classical chips handle logic. Quantum processors perform sub-tasks that benefit from parallelism, such as optimizing motion paths or simulating materials. Companies already build hybrid software bridges that let developers combine both resources (IBM Research, 2024).

The same approach that accelerates chemistry will eventually accelerate robotics.

Invest AI Viewpoint

Quantum computing is the silent accelerator behind the robotics boom. It will not replace GPUs or CPUs but make them smarter. Quantum simulations will shorten prototype cycles and improve resource efficiency. The leaders will be those who control both hardware and algorithm, blending AI, robotics, and quantum architecture into a unified system.

Investor Takeaways

Track public quantum companies such as IBM (IBM), D-Wave Quantum (QBTS), Rigetti (RGTI), and IonQ (IONQ).
Follow large cloud providers such as Amazon (AMZN), Microsoft (MSFT), and Google (GOOGL) for quantum-as-a-service exposure.
Watch materials firms using quantum modeling to build robotic parts or batteries. Consider venture funds and ETFs that balance AI and quantum equities. Treat this sector as long horizon, with slow adoption but high long-term potential.

# 4

# The Industrial Stack: How AI and Robotics Are Rebuilding the Global Factory

Every robot runs on a hidden backbone of machines, sensors, and software. This backbone is called the industrial stack. It is the layer where artificial intelligence meets the real world. Without it, no robot can move, weld, or deliver a product.

Understanding the Layers

Think of the industrial stack as a living circuit. At the bottom are the power systems and motors. Above them sit the controllers that tell each part what to do. On top of that are the sensors, vision systems, and software that help robots make decisions.

When a factory robot places a microchip or a humanoid walks across a floor, each motion passes through these layers in milliseconds. Data moves from sensors to processors to actuators in a continuous loop. Every layer must work in perfect sync.

Industrial automation companies design and sell these layers as integrated ecosystems. ABB, Siemens, and Rockwell Automation have spent decades connecting hardware with control software. Newer entrants such as Omron and Schneider Electric are adding AI-driven analytics to predict failures and optimize workflows (McKinsey & Company, 2024).

## The Heart of Automation

The central control systems of factories are called programmable logic controllers, or PLCs. They are the nervous system of the industrial stack. Modern PLCs are merging with AI modules that allow self-tuning and fault prediction. This means machines can adjust themselves before something breaks, saving time and cost.

Motion control is another essential layer. Companies such as Yaskawa Electric and FANUC make servo motors that deliver precise torque and speed. These components give robots smooth, human-like motion. Meanwhile, sensor firms including Keyence, Cognex, and SICK AG provide vision and awareness.

As these parts connect through digital twins and simulation software, the industrial stack becomes a digital organism. It can model, test, and perfect production before a single part is made.

## The AI Layer

Artificial intelligence now sits at the top of this stack. Machine learning helps predict demand, schedule maintenance, and even design new parts. In smart factories, AI uses real-time data to decide when to slow a line, reroute a task, or order new materials.

According to Deloitte (2024), manufacturers using integrated AI and automation systems see up to twenty percent higher output and fifteen percent lower downtime. The global industrial automation market is projected to exceed four hundred billion U.S. dollars by 2030 (Mordor Intelligence, 2025).

Data and Connectivity

Connectivity ties the layers together. Industrial Internet of Things platforms, known as IIoT, such as Siemens MindSphere and ABB Ability, link machines, sensors, and analytics dashboards. This constant data flow allows plant managers to view performance from anywhere. It also creates new markets for predictive software and cybersecurity, since each connected robot becomes a data node.

Fifth-generation networks and edge computing enhance this even further. With faster data transmission and local processing, latency falls and decision speed rises. Robots can now respond in real time without relying on distant cloud servers.

Invest AI Viewpoint

The industrial stack is the skeleton of the machine economy. It is where old industries learn to think. Every advance in robotics or AI depends on these hidden systems of power, motion, sensing, and control. Investors who understand this foundation can recognize value before it appears on the surface.

Investor Takeaways

Watch industrial leaders such as ABB (ABBN.SW), Siemens (SIE.DE), Rockwell Automation (ROK), and Schneider Electric (SU.PA). Study automation suppliers such as Omron (6645.T) and Yaskawa Electric (6506.T). Follow vision and sensor specialists such as Cognex (CGNX), Keyence (6861.T), and SICK AG (SICK.DE). Explore IIoT and digital twin providers including Siemens MindSphere, ABB Ability, PTC, and Dassault Systèmes. Research

ETFs that include industrial automation and smart manufacturing exposure.

# 5

# The Rise of Humanoid Robots: Building Factories of One in the Age of AI

The idea of a humanoid robot has lived in science fiction for more than a century. Today, it is a business plan. Across labs in the United States, China, and Japan, engineers are building robots that look and move like people. These machines are no longer fantasy. They are prototypes preparing for factories, warehouses, and service industries.

The Rise of General-Purpose Robots

Traditional industrial robots perform a single task such as welding, packaging, or assembly. Humanoids are designed to do many. They can pick, carry, balance, and even use tools made for human hands. Their advantage is flexibility. They can learn multiple roles without changing the factory layout.

Companies such as Figure AI, Agility Robotics, and Sanctuary AI are leading this race. Figure's humanoid robot, Figure 01, can walk, lift, and manipulate objects with precision. Agility's Digit robot already operates in pilot programs for logistics and retail partners (Agility Robotics, 2024). Sanctuary's Phoenix model performs cognitive tasks such as sorting or labeling.

Japanese companies including Toyota, Honda, and SoftBank Robotics continue to push design boundaries. Their goal is to create humanoids that work in aging societies and healthcare systems where labor shortages are rising.

## Factories of One

The next phase of manufacturing is the Factory of One. In this model, a humanoid robot becomes a self-contained production unit. Each machine carries its own sensors, software, and tools to perform small-batch manufacturing or specialized repair.

This trend reduces the need for large centralized factories. A network of humanoid workers can perform production tasks locally, increasing flexibility and reducing logistics costs. According to McKinsey (2024), modular and decentralized manufacturing could raise efficiency by up to thirty percent while cutting energy use by twenty percent.

## The Technical Challenge

Building a humanoid is complex. The main barrier is control. A human body uses more than six hundred muscles. Reproducing even a fraction of that coordination requires advanced sensors, actuators, and learning models. Power density and battery life also limit performance. Companies are exploring new materials and joint mechanisms to solve these problems (IEEE Spectrum, 2024).

Cloud-based AI training helps. Robots can share data, learning from each other's experiences. When one humanoid learns to pick up a box, another can copy that motion instantly through software updates. This collective learning approach makes every new robot smarter than the last.

The Economic Shift

Humanoids could redefine labor economics. Early models cost hundreds of thousands of dollars, but as production scales, costs will fall. Analysts estimate that by 2035, a general-purpose humanoid could cost less than a year's wage for a skilled worker (Goldman Sachs, 2023). This makes humanoids not a replacement, but a supplement to the global workforce.

Governments are beginning to prepare. Japan, South Korea, and the European Union have drafted ethical frameworks and worker adaptation plans. In the United States, industrial humanoids are now part of Department of Energy-funded pilot programs exploring automation in logistics and energy sectors (Department of Energy, 2024).

Invest AI Viewpoint

Humanoids represent the bridge between automation and autonomy. They can fill jobs where humans are scarce, perform dangerous tasks, and extend human capability into new environments. We believe humanoids will become the defining image of physical AI by the mid-2030s. The market will expand from industrial prototypes to retail, logistics, and domestic assistance. Investors should view humanoids as the natural progression of industrial robotics and machine learning. The companies building them today may define the next trillion-dollar industrial category.

Investor Takeaways

Track private leaders such as Figure AI, Agility Robotics, Sanctuary AI, and Apptronik.
Watch large public firms funding humanoid R&D, including Toyota (7203.T), Honda (7267.T), and Hyundai (005380.KS). Study suppliers of actuators, batteries, and lightweight materials that enable humanoid mobility. Follow AI-chip developers such as NVIDIA (NVDA) and AMD (AMD) whose

processors train and run humanoid control systems. Look for ETFs or funds that include robotics and automation exposure, such as BOTZ and IRBO.

# 6

# Investing in Robotics: Public Leaders and Private Frontrunners Building the Machine Economy

Investing in robotics means understanding who builds the future and who funds it. Some companies already dominate public markets, while others quietly shape tomorrow's breakthroughs behind closed doors. Together, they form the foundation of the robotics economy.

**The Public Leaders**

Publicly traded robotics and automation companies have become the backbone of modern industry. They design machines, sensors, software, and infrastructure. These are the companies most investors can access directly through stock markets or ETFs.

According to Mordor Intelligence (2025), the global robotics sector will exceed 185 billion U.S. dollars by 2030, with steady annual growth near twenty percent. That growth comes from industrial automation, logistics robotics, and AI integration.

Key public players include:

- ABB (ABBN.SW): A Swiss pioneer in industrial automation, robotics, and electrification. ABB's robots are used in automotive, electronics, and healthcare sectors.
- Siemens (SIE.DE): A global leader in control systems, smart factories, and Industrial Internet of Things platforms such as MindSphere.
- Rockwell Automation (ROK): A U.S.-based automation specialist providing hardware and software for advanced manufacturing.
- FANUC (6954.T): A Japanese robotics giant with strong market share in assembly and motion-control systems.
- Yaskawa Electric (6506.T): Produces servo motors and industrial robots across Asia and Europe.
- Keyence (6861.T) and Cognex (CGNX): Leaders in vision systems and sensors that help robots see and identify objects.
- Symbotic (SYM): Focused on warehouse and logistics automation, partnered with large retailers to optimize supply chains.
- Intuitive Surgical (ISRG): Creator of the da Vinci surgical system, blending robotics with healthcare innovation.
- NVIDIA (NVDA): The computing powerhouse behind AI chips that train and run robotic systems in real time.

These companies form the stable, long-term foundation of the robotics investment universe.

**The Private Frontrunners**

Private robotics startups drive innovation faster than traditional giants. They are the source of new designs, fresh markets, and experimental technology. Many of these companies will go public or be acquired within the next decade.

Prominent private players include:

- Figure AI: Developer of humanoid robots for industrial and service environments.
- Agility Robotics: Maker of Digit, one of the first general-purpose humanoids operating in warehouse logistics.
- Sanctuary AI: Combines cognitive AI models with physical robotics, creating adaptive humanoid systems.
- Apptronik: Focused on lightweight exoskeletons and humanoid robotics for industrial use.
- Fourier Intelligence (China): Produces rehabilitation robots and exosuits for medical applications.
- NEURA Robotics (Germany): Designs collaborative robots, or cobots, for small-business manufacturing.
- Boston Dynamics: Famous for Spot and Atlas robots, advancing agility and perception across terrains.

These startups raise funding from venture firms such as Andreessen Horowitz, Sequoia Capital, and OpenAI's investment partners (Crunchbase, 2025).

The Emerging Middle Layer

Between the large industrial leaders and small startups lies a new middle market. These firms supply key components; sensors, processors, and materials, that make robotics possible. Examples include Teledyne Technologies (TDY), Basler AG (BSL.DE), and Luminar Technologies (LAZR), which produce machine vision and LiDAR systems.

The companies in this tier may not be household names, but they often provide the highest growth potential because their technology becomes industry standard. Investors can monitor them through quarterly reports and technology-integration news from larger firms.

Market Strategy

Investors can mix large, stable robotics companies with smaller innovators for a balanced portfolio. The large firms provide long-term growth and dividends. The smaller or private companies represent potential for exponential return once they scale or go public.

Analysts often recommend maintaining a seventy-thirty ratio between established and emerging robotics exposure for a moderate-risk strategy (Deloitte, 2024).

Invest AI Viewpoint

The robotics ecosystem mirrors the early days of the internet: a few giants build the foundation while thousands of smaller innovators race to fill new niches. Our analysis suggests that mergers, acquisitions, and IPOs will define the next decade. Private humanoid and logistics robotics companies will either partner with or be purchased by major industrial players.

Investors should treat the robotics sector like a living network, where innovation constantly moves from startup to conglomerate. Those who follow this flow and adjust early will be ahead of the curve.

Investor Takeaways

- Watch leading industrial automation stocks; ABB, Siemens, Rockwell, FANUC, and Yaskawa.
- Study component and sensor companies; Keyence, Cognex, Basler, and Luminar.
- Follow private innovators; Figure AI, Agility Robotics, Sanctuary AI, and NEURA Robotics.
- Track upcoming IPO announcements in humanoid and logistics robotics sectors.
- Diversify across public ETFs such as ROBO, BOTZ, and IRBO for broad exposure.

# 7

# The Supply Chain of Intelligence: How AI and Robotics Are Powering the Next Industrial Revolution

Every robot is a system of systems. To understand how to invest in robotics, you must first understand the supply chain that brings intelligence to life. This chain links sensors, chips, motors, software, and power. Each part is a business on its own, and each step creates opportunities for investors.

**The Hidden Infrastructure**

When people think about robots, they often imagine humanoids or mechanical arms. But behind every moving machine is a global network of suppliers. A single autonomous robot can depend on hundreds of components made by companies across Asia, Europe, and North America.

The base of the supply chain starts with semiconductors; the processors that power the brain of every robot. These chips run perception, planning, and control. Leaders in this space include NVIDIA, AMD, Intel, and STMicroelectronics (McKinsey & Company, 2024). Their AI accelerators are now standard in drones, factory robots, and autonomous vehicles.

The next layer is sensing and perception. Robots need to see and understand the world, which means cameras, LiDAR, radar, and ultrasonic sensors. Companies like Cognex (CGNX) and Keyence (6861.T) lead in machine vision. Luminar (LAZR), Hesai (HSAI), and Innoviz (INVZ) develop LiDAR sensors that map space in three dimensions. These systems are essential for both industrial automation and self-driving technology (Mordor Intelligence, 2025).

After sensing comes motion and control. Here, companies such as FANUC (6954.T), Yaskawa Electric (6506.T), Harmonic Drive (6324.T), and THK (6481.T) supply actuators, servos, and linear drives. These mechanical parts translate digital signals into movement.

Next is power and energy. Battery providers like BYD (1211.HK) and CATL (300750.SZ) design compact cells to give mobile robots and humanoids longer working hours. Meanwhile, companies like Vicor (VICR) and Infineon Technologies (IFX.DE) produce modules that regulate power delivery for precision and safety.

At the top of the chain is software integration. Companies such as PTC (PTC), Dassault Systèmes (DSY.PA), and Unity Technologies (U) build simulation and design environments for robotics systems. These "digital twin" platforms allow engineers to test machines virtually before they build them in the real world (Deloitte, 2024).

**The Importance of Interoperability**

The robotics supply chain only works if these components speak the same language. Standardization, open APIs, and ROS 2 (Robot Operating System) make this possible. Open-source ecosystems reduce cost and accelerate innovation. Many startups now design hardware compatible with ROS 2 to reach wider markets.

Investors should note that interoperability creates long-term winners. Firms that set standards or supply software widely adopted by others tend to dominate their category.

**Regional Clusters**

- Asia: Japan and China lead in motion systems and sensors. Taiwan dominates semiconductor fabrication.
- Europe: Germany and Switzerland lead in automation equipment and metrology.
- United States: Leads in AI chip design, simulation software, and humanoid robotics.

Tracking regional clusters helps investors understand where supply shortages or breakthroughs might occur. For example, chip fabrication bottlenecks in Taiwan can affect global robotics production timelines.

**The Resilience Factor**

The COVID-19 pandemic revealed how fragile global supply chains can be. Since then, major robotics firms have invested in reshoring; moving production closer to home markets, and vertical integration, where companies own more of their own supply chain. This trend protects profit margins and reduces risk. It also creates new investment opportunities in logistics robotics, 3D printing, and local manufacturing hubs (Deloitte, 2024).

**Invest AI Viewpoint**

The supply chain is where the robotics revolution quietly happens. It is less glamorous than humanoids, but it holds steady growth and lower volatility. We believe the next wave of value will come from suppliers that make intelligence scalable; companies producing sensors, chips, and power systems that every robot requires. These are the "picks and shovels" of the machine age.

**Investor Takeaways**

- Follow semiconductor leaders: NVIDIA (NVDA), AMD (AMD), Intel (INTC), and STMicroelectronics (STM).
- Track LiDAR and sensor innovators: Luminar (LAZR), Hesai (HSAI), Innoviz (INVZ), Cognex (CGNX), and Keyence (6861.T).
- Study motion and actuator companies: FANUC (6954.T), Yaskawa (6506.T), Harmonic Drive (6324.T), and THK (6481.T).
- Watch power and energy suppliers: BYD (1211.HK), CATL (300750.SZ), Vicor (VICR), and Infineon (IFX.DE).
- Research digital twin and simulation firms: PTC (PTC), Dassault Systèmes (DSY.PA), and Unity Technologies (U).
- Diversify exposure with robotics and automation ETFs (ROBO, BOTZ, IRBO).

# 8

# Robotic Software and Simulation Economies: How AI and Digital Twins Are Building the Brains of Automation

Robots are built from metal and code. The metal gives them strength. The code gives them thought. Software and simulation are what turn hardware into intelligence. Without these tools, robots could not plan, adapt, or improve.

## The Digital Twin Revolution

A digital twin is a virtual copy of a real system. It lets engineers test designs, simulate motion, and fix problems before building anything physical. In robotics, digital twins shorten development time and lower cost. They also make continuous improvement possible.

For example, Siemens and PTC build digital twin software that models entire factories. NVIDIA's Isaac Sim and Unity's Simulation Pro can model how robots see and move through space (NVIDIA, 2024). Engineers use these simulations to train AI models that control motion and avoid collisions.

According to Deloitte (2024), companies that adopt simulation and twin technology reduce prototyping costs by up to thirty percent and increase deployment speed by nearly twenty-five percent. That efficiency becomes a measurable investment advantage.

## Software as the Nervous System

Software manages every layer of robotics: vision, movement, communication, and data analysis. Some of the most valuable robotics companies are actually software firms that control hardware built by others.

PTC (PTC) offers Creo and ThingWorx, tools for digital design and IoT integration. Dassault Systèmes (DSY.PA) provides CATIA and 3DEXPERIENCE, used to design robots, vehicles, and production lines. Autodesk (ADSK) specializes in 3D modeling and is now expanding into AI-assisted design.

Simulation software also drives robotics training. AI models need millions of practice runs to learn. Doing this in the real world would take months. In simulation, it takes hours. Platforms such as NVIDIA Omniverse and Unity Robotics Hub use physics-based rendering to create realistic virtual environments for robot learning.

## Data Is the Fuel

Every robot creates data: camera feeds, temperature readings, motor speeds, and position coordinates. Software companies convert that data into insight. Predictive analytics identifies weak parts before they fail. Cloud dashboards let managers control hundreds of robots remotely.

Amazon Web Services (AWS) and Microsoft Azure host entire robotics operations through cloud APIs. These systems provide scalability and security while collecting data that improves performance over time (McKinsey &

Company, 2024).

The Economics of Software

Software brings recurring revenue. Unlike hardware, which sells once, software licenses renew monthly or yearly. This creates steady cash flow and high margins. As automation spreads, the demand for integration software grows across every industry.

Investors should note that while hardware companies dominate headlines, software firms often produce higher returns. Their scalability is nearly unlimited once platforms are established.

Invest AI Viewpoint

The real value of robotics is not in the robot itself but in the intelligence that controls it. The companies that build simulation and control software hold the keys to efficiency and scale. We believe software and digital-twin ecosystems will become the backbone of every robotics operation. The firms that control data, integration, and learning pipelines will lead the next wave of automation profits.

Investor Takeaways

- Follow simulation leaders such as NVIDIA (NVDA), PTC (PTC), Dassault Systèmes (DSY.PA), Unity Technologies (U), and Autodesk (ADSK). Watch cloud providers offering robotics platforms such as Amazon (AMZN), Microsoft (MSFT), and Google (GOOGL).
- Study firms developing AI-training environments such as NVIDIA Omniverse and Unity Robotics Hub.
- Evaluate industrial-software ETFs or funds focused on digital manufacturing and IoT.
- Track private startups building AI-assisted design or simulation-as-a-

service products.

# 9

# The Future of 3D Printing: On-Demand Manufacturing in the Age of Robotics and Automation

## 3D Printing and On-Demand Manufacture

Every industrial revolution begins with a new way to make things. For robotics, that method is 3D printing, also known as additive manufacturing. It allows companies to create parts, tools, and even entire robotic systems on demand.

## The Role of Additive Manufacturing in Robotics

Traditional manufacturing cuts material away to form parts. Additive manufacturing builds them layer by layer from digital files. This process saves material, reduces waste, and enables designs that were once impossible.

Robotics companies use 3D printing to prototype gears, joints, and housings. Engineers can print a new design, test it within hours, and modify it instantly. According to Grand View Research (2025), the global additive manufacturing market is expected to reach more than eighty-four billion U.S. dollars by

2030.

That growth reflects how manufacturing itself is changing. Small production runs, custom robotics, and rapid iteration are now more efficient than mass production.

## How 3D Printing Supports Automation

Robotics and 3D printing are deeply connected. Robots assemble products, and 3D printers create the parts robots use. In advanced factories, the two systems operate together. Robots manage print farms, remove parts, and conduct quality control using vision sensors.

Companies such as Stratasys (SSYS) and 3D Systems (DDD) lead industrial printing. Markforged (MKFG) specializes in carbon-fiber composites that make robotic arms lighter and stronger. Desktop Metal (DM) develops metal-based printing for end-use parts.

Some robotics companies even build their own printers to produce components in-house. This reduces shipping time and lowers reliance on external suppliers.

## Materials and Innovation

Additive manufacturing is not limited to plastic. Metal, carbon fiber, and ceramics can now be printed with high precision. In robotics, lightweight strength is critical. Advanced composites improve speed and energy efficiency.

Nano Dimension (NNDM) prints electronic circuits directly into mechanical parts, merging hardware and electronics. Protolabs (PRLB) and Xometry (XMTR) offer on-demand manufacturing platforms where customers upload digital designs and receive finished components in days.

These services make high-tech fabrication accessible to startups and research labs that cannot afford large factories.

## The Economics of On-Demand Production

On-demand manufacturing replaces inventory with data. Instead of storing thousands of spare parts, companies store digital design files. When a part is needed, they print it locally. This approach reduces waste, shipping costs, and carbon emissions.

According to Deloitte (2024), companies adopting additive manufacturing for spare-part logistics can cut inventory costs by forty percent and lead time by sixty percent. That efficiency gives robotics firms a measurable competitive advantage.

## The Future of Localized Manufacturing

As supply chains become more digital, the future may favor micro-factories, small automated sites that produce goods where they are needed. These factories can combine robotics, AI, and 3D printing to manufacture custom products at scale.

Governments and corporations are investing heavily in localized production to reduce dependence on global shipping. The European Union, Japan, and the United States are funding additive manufacturing hubs that train workers and test new materials (European Commission, 2024).

## Invest AI Viewpoint

3D printing turns every robotics company into its own factory. It gives startups and established firms the power to innovate faster and control their supply chain. We believe additive manufacturing will be a key enabler of the robotics economy. It bridges design, production, and repair, making machines more adaptable and affordable.

Investor Takeaways

- Follow 3D printing leaders such as Stratasys (SSYS), 3D Systems (DDD), Markforged (MKFG), and Desktop Metal (DM).
- Track electronics and advanced materials innovators such as Nano Dimension (NNDM), Protolabs (PRLB), and Xometry (XMTR).
- Watch additive manufacturing ETFs such as PRNT for diversified exposure.
- Research partnerships between robotics firms and printing companies in automotive and aerospace.
- Observe government initiatives in additive manufacturing hubs for long-term policy support.

# 10

# Crypto Infrastructure and DePIN Markets: How Blockchain, AI, and Robotics Are Building the Machine Economy

The rise of intelligent machines is not only about hardware and AI. It is also about how these machines connect, share data, and trade resources. A new frontier called DePIN, short for Decentralized Physical Infrastructure Networks, links robotics, AI, and crypto technology into one shared economy. It's where the physical and digital worlds start to earn together.

**What Is DePIN?**

In a DePIN system, physical devices; such as sensors, drones, or robots, connect to a blockchain network. Each device contributes something valuable, such as data, computing power, or location services, and earns digital tokens in return (Messari, 2025).

Think of it as the "internet of machines," where devices exchange value directly. No middleman, no centralized cloud. Each participant; human or machine, owns part of the infrastructure it helps build.

This model allows investors, developers, and everyday users to co-own and fund real-world systems like computing, mapping, connectivity, and energy through decentralized participation.

### Why Robotics Needs Blockchain

*Robotics and AI require trusted data, reliable coordination, and secure payments. Blockchains provide those capabilities natively.*

- Data Security: Distributed ledgers make it nearly impossible to alter or falsify sensor data, improving transparency and safety in robotics.
- Autonomous Payments: Robots and vehicles can pay each other automatically for services using crypto tokens.
- Traceability: Every transaction is recorded on-chain, creating auditable histories for logistics, energy, or maintenance operations.

Example: a delivery drone recharges at a solar station and pays instantly in tokens; a self-driving car sells its traffic data to a mapping network; a humanoid robot rents extra compute power from a decentralized GPU cluster.

This turns machines into economic agents; self-sustaining entities that earn, spend, and maintain themselves without human supervision.

### Leading DePIN Projects

Several pioneering projects are already connecting physical infrastructure to blockchain networks:

- Hivemapper: Builds a decentralized Google Maps alternative. Drivers attach cameras, capture street-level footage, and earn tokens for contributing new data.
- DIMO: Gathers real-time vehicle telemetry for developers, insurance

firms, and fleet operators.

- Render Network (RNDR): Allows GPU owners to share unused computing power for AI training, 3D rendering, and robotics simulation (Render Foundation, 2024).
- Akash Network (AKT): Offers decentralized cloud computing where developers rent CPU and GPU power through smart contracts.
- Bittensor (TAO): Creates a marketplace where AI models exchange knowledge, compute, and data in exchange for tokens.
- Filecoin and Arweave: Provide decentralized storage used by AI and robotics firms to archive massive training datasets.

According to Binance Research (2024), if adoption continues across mobility, data, and compute sectors, DePIN markets could surpass 3 trillion U.S. dollars in value by 2040.

**The Convergence with AI and Robotics**

AI systems need enormous amounts of data and computing power. Robotics generates that data through sensors, cameras, and movement. DePIN connects the two by decentralizing the physical infrastructure that powers them.

- **Robots contribute data.**
- **AI models consume and refine it.**
- **Blockchains record, reward, and distribute the value.**

This allows AI and robotic systems to cooperate globally without relying solely on Big Tech data centers. As autonomy increases, robots will participate in decentralized economies—buying compute power, selling data, and negotiating microtransactions in real time.

This is where robotics meets finance: physical systems operating as financial participants.

**How Investors Can Participate Early**

DePIN is still young, but you don't need to be a coder to invest or participate. Here are accessible entry points:

1. Token Exposure (Beginner Path):

Buy small amounts of tokens from major DePIN projects such as RNDR (Render Network), AKT (Akash), TAO (Bittensor), FIL (Filecoin), and AR (Arweave). Always use reputable exchanges and secure your crypto in a hardware wallet. These tokens often represent network participation and reward distribution.

2. Node or Device Participation (Intermediate Path):

Some networks allow users to contribute hardware and earn rewards. For example:

- Run a Render Node by sharing unused GPU power.
- Operate an Akash Provider to rent spare server capacity.
- Install a Hivemapper Dashcam to earn tokens by mapping your city.
- These are hands-on ways to own a small piece of the infrastructure itself.

3. Infrastructure Investing (Advanced Path):

Support startups and hardware manufacturers building robotics–blockchain integrations. Some early-stage funds and DAOs (Decentralized Autonomous Organizations) focus entirely on DePIN projects. Accredited investors can also seek private placements in emerging networks or equity rounds tied to hardware and data companies.

4. Build or Partner (Founder Path):

Use the Native Markets Builder Framework to create your own DePIN-connected app or prototype. As shown in Building for the Native Markets, A Founder's Guide, even non-technical founders can use AI tools like ChatGPT, Replit, and Bubble to prototype new systems that connect physical devices to blockchain networks.

This could mean a DePIN dashboard, AI monitoring agent, or marketplace that visualizes network activity and token rewards.

**The Risk and Reward Profile**

- DePIN sits at the frontier of regulation and technology. The risks include:
- Regulatory Uncertainty: Global crypto laws are still forming.
- Technical Complexity: Networks must handle real-world hardware failures.
- Market Volatility: Tokens can fluctuate wildly in early stages.

Yet the upside is unprecedented. DePIN represents a new category of infrastructure investment, where individuals can co-own global networks that previously required billions in capital. Just as early internet users once hosted websites, DePIN participants can now host compute, data, or mobility nodes.

If cloud computing powered the 2010s, distributed physical infrastructure could define the 2030s.

**Invest AI Viewpoint**

DePIN represents the missing economic layer for autonomous systems. It transforms machines from passive tools into active participants that earn and exchange value.

We believe the convergence of robotics, AI, and blockchain will define the financial backbone of the intelligent world.

The firms and projects that build these decentralized rails will become the next generation of infrastructure titans; akin to the Amazons and Googles of the past internet era, but owned by their users.

Investor Takeaways

- Study DePIN projects with proven real-world utility: Hivemapper, DIMO, Render, Akash, Bittensor, Filecoin, and Arweave.
- Watch for hardware-to-blockchain integrations from major robotics and AI companies.
- Treat DePIN tokens as speculative infrastructure exposure; diversify across multiple networks.
- Follow GPU and data-infrastructure firms that enable decentralized compute, such as NVIDIA and AMD.
- Track policy developments on crypto infrastructure and data sovereignty to anticipate mainstream adoption.

# 11

# Japan: Precision and Motion Mastery: How the Nation Became the Global Powerhouse of Robotics.

Japan is the quiet heartbeat of global robotics. For decades, it has combined discipline, engineering, and efficiency to become the world's most consistent producer of industrial robots. Its approach to robotics reflects the culture that built it; focused, methodical, and committed to mastery.

**The Birthplace of Modern Robotics**

Japan's robotics history began after World War II, when automation became essential for rebuilding its economy. The first generation of robots, developed by companies like Kawasaki Heavy Industries (7012.T) and FANUC (6954.T), were created to support manufacturing and automotive assembly.

By the 1980s, Japan controlled more than half of the global industrial robot market. Its philosophy was precision over speed. This mindset shaped the entire industry. Where others chased innovation, Japan perfected execution.

Today, that precision continues. The International Federation of Robotics (2024) reports that Japan produces nearly half of the world's industrial robots. Its companies lead in servo motors, sensors, and automation software.

## Precision Engineering and Motion Control

Japanese robotics companies excel in motion systems; the parts that make robots move smoothly and safely. Yaskawa Electric (6506.T) and Nidec (6594.T) dominate servo and micro-motor manufacturing. Harmonic Drive (6324.T) supplies precision gears used in space robotics, surgery, and humanoid locomotion.

In automation, Omron (6645.T) and Keyence (6861.T) drive innovation in factory sensors and machine vision. Their systems are known for reliability and accuracy, powering assembly lines across the world.

Japan's advantage lies in its supply chain synergy. Companies cooperate rather than compete, sharing components and design standards that ensure compatibility and stability. This creates a robust industrial ecosystem where parts from different firms fit together seamlessly.

## Robotics Meets Society

Japan faces an aging population and labor shortages. Rather than replacing workers, robots fill essential roles. Healthcare, logistics, and elder care are major areas of deployment.

SoftBank Robotics gained global attention with the humanoid assistant Pepper, designed to interact with people in public spaces. Toyota and Honda are developing humanoid and assistive robots that help with lifting, mobility, and daily care (Toyota Research Institute, 2024).

Government policy supports this shift. Japan's "Society 5.0" initiative aims to blend digital and physical systems into a single, human-centered society. Robotics, AI, and IoT form the backbone of this vision (Government of Japan, 2024).

**Export Strength and Global Reach**

Japan exports robots to every major manufacturing region. The country's machines operate in factories across the United States, Europe, and China.

Japanese robots are valued not only for technology but for reliability. In robotics, downtime costs money. Japan's reputation for consistency keeps it ahead of many lower-cost producers.

The nation's industrial base also supports international collaborations. FANUC and ABB (ABBN.SW) operate joint ventures, while Yaskawa partners with German firms to combine mechanical expertise with European AI software.

**Research and Innovation**

Universities and research institutions play a central role in Japan's robotics dominance. The University of Tokyo, Osaka University, and Riken Center for Intelligent Systems lead global studies in motion planning, humanoid balance, and tactile sensing.

Startups such as Preferred Networks work with Toyota to integrate AI into industrial robots, using deep learning to improve flexibility and decision-making. Japan's robotics ecosystem extends from high school competitions to world-class labs — a complete educational pipeline for talent and innovation.

**Invest AI Viewpoint**

Japan represents the steady, engineering-first model of the robotics revolution. While Silicon Valley often moves fast and breaks things, Japan moves deliberately and builds systems that last. Investors should view Japanese robotics firms as the backbone of global automation; stable, export-driven, and quietly profitable.

Japan's long-term value lies not in flashy humanoids but in motion systems, sensors, and control technologies that every robot on Earth depends on.

**Investor Takeaways**

- Track leading Japanese automation firms: FANUC (6954.T), Yaskawa Electric (6506.T), Omron (6645.T), and Keyence (6861.T).
- Watch precision engineering companies: Nidec (6594.T) and Harmonic Drive (6324.T).
- Follow humanoid and service robotics developers: Toyota, Honda, and SoftBank Robotics.
- Monitor ETFs with Japan automation exposure such as EWJ, FJP, and BOTZ.
- Study government policies like "Society 5.0" for insights into state-backed innovation.

# 12

# United States: AI and Humanoid Frontiers: How America Leads the Global Robotics Revolution

The United States sits at the intersection of imagination and engineering. It is where the dream of artificial intelligence became a trillion-dollar economy and where the next frontier, humanoid robotics, is taking shape. America's robotics revolution is fueled by venture capital, big data, and an entrepreneurial culture that treats technology as destiny.

## The Power of Innovation

U.S. robotics thrives because of its innovation pipeline. Startups can move from concept to funding faster than anywhere else. Venture firms, research universities, and corporate investors form a cycle that transforms ideas into industries.

The United States leads in AI software, autonomous vehicles, defense robotics, and humanoid development. According to McKinsey & Company (2024), nearly forty percent of global robotics venture funding flows to American firms. This concentration of capital attracts top engineers from around the world.

## The Humanoid Race

No other country matches the United States in humanoid experimentation. Figure AI, based in California, is developing a general-purpose humanoid called Figure 01 for manufacturing and logistics. Agility Robotics, from Oregon, built the bipedal robot Digit, which now operates in warehouse pilot programs for major retailers. Apptronik, headquartered in Texas, focuses on lightweight humanoids designed for industrial and service environments.

- Each company represents a different philosophy:
- Figure AI aims for large-scale, factory-level deployment.
- Agility Robotics targets logistics and warehouse automation.
- Apptronik develops humanoids for direct human collaboration.

The U.S. humanoid sector benefits from rapid prototyping, AI chip availability, and strong partnerships with cloud providers such as Amazon and Microsoft.

## Defense and Aerospace Robotics

The American defense sector has driven robotics research for decades through programs at DARPA, NASA, and the Department of Defense. Autonomous drones, bomb-disposal units, and planetary rovers all originated from this ecosystem.

NASA's Valkyrie humanoid project and the Jet Propulsion Laboratory's autonomous systems have influenced modern commercial robot design (NASA, 2024). Boston Dynamics, born from DARPA funding, remains a global benchmark for mobility and balance. Its robots Spot and Atlas demonstrate how software and mechanics can combine to achieve near-human agility.

Industrial and Logistics Automation

In industrial robotics, U.S. companies focus on productivity and software integration. Teradyne (TER), through its subsidiary Universal Robots, dominates the collaborative robot, or "cobot," market. Symbotic (SYM) automates warehouse logistics for retail giants such as Walmart.

In automotive manufacturing, Tesla (TSLA) integrates robotics into every production line and is developing the Optimus humanoid for future automation. The company's real-world AI model, trained through its vehicle fleet, may eventually guide physical robots (Tesla, 2024).

Academic and Research Hubs

American universities form the foundation of robotics innovation. MIT, Stanford, Carnegie Mellon, and Georgia Tech lead research on robot learning, dexterity, and human-machine interaction.

The National Science Foundation and the Department of Energy fund robotics and AI research across manufacturing, energy, and national security (Department of Energy, 2024). This steady public investment ensures progress even when private funding slows.

The AI Advantage

The United States dominates artificial intelligence infrastructure. OpenAI, NVIDIA, Google DeepMind, and Anthropic create the models and hardware that drive global machine learning. This vertical integration between software and physical systems gives U.S. robotics firms a decisive edge. Robots built in America often run AI trained on domestic cloud networks, ensuring security, speed, and regulatory compliance.

According to Deloitte (2024), integrating AI with physical automation could raise U.S. industrial output by fifteen percent over the next decade. This synergy between AI and robotics defines America's competitive advantage.

Invest AI Viewpoint

The United States represents the creative frontier of robotics. It leads in AI, humanoid design, and cloud infrastructure. Its approach is bold, fast, and risk-tolerant. While volatility is inevitable, innovation returns remain unmatched.

We believe American robotics firms will continue to lead in humanoid form factors, software integration, and AI-driven automation. The ecosystem; from venture funding to university research, remains the deepest and most dynamic in the world.

Investor Takeaways

- Watch humanoid innovators: Figure AI, Agility Robotics, Apptronik, and Boston Dynamics.
- Track industrial automation leaders: Teradyne (TER), Symbotic (SYM), and Tesla (TSLA).
- Follow AI platform providers shaping robotics intelligence: NVIDIA (NVDA), Microsoft (MSFT), and Google (GOOGL).
- Study ETFs offering U.S. automation exposure: ROBO, IRBO, and BOTZ.
- Monitor defense and aerospace robotics programs under DARPA and NASA for early innovation signals.

# 13

# China: Scale and LiDAR Dominance

## China: Scale and LiDAR Dominance

If Japan is the master of precision, China is the master of scale. Its robotics sector is expanding faster than any other in the world, powered by government policy, manufacturing expertise, and national ambition. In China, robotics is not just an industry; it is a pillar of national strategy.

### The Scale of a Nation

China has made robotics central to its economic transformation. Under the Made in China 2025 plan, the government aims to lead the world in advanced manufacturing, automation, and AI (State Council of China, 2024). Billions of dollars in state and private funding flow annually into robotics startups, research centers, and industrial automation projects.

The International Federation of Robotics (2024) reports that China installs more industrial robots each year than any other nation—more than half of the global total. Scale has turned automation from a competitive edge into a basic requirement of Chinese manufacturing.

### The LiDAR Advantage

China dominates LiDAR production, the laser-based technology that helps robots and autonomous vehicles map and navigate their surroundings. Leading companies include Hesai Technology (HSAI), RoboSense (002813.SZ), and Innovusion, which supply sensors to global automakers and robotics firms.

This leadership is built on two strengths: optical precision and mass manufacturing. Chinese factories can produce LiDAR sensors at a fraction of the cost of Western competitors, enabling widespread adoption across robotics, mobility, and logistics. Affordable sensors are what turned China into the engine room of the global autonomous-vehicle supply chain.

Industrial Automation and Manufacturing Power

China's industrial champions; Siasun Robot (300024.SZ), Estun Automation (002747.SZ), and EFORT Intelligent Equipment (688165.SS), build robots for electronics, automotive, and heavy industry. These firms often collaborate with Japanese and European partners, combining imported components with domestic AI software to improve reliability and performance.

Foreign automation giants such as ABB, Siemens, and FANUC also operate major production hubs in China. This collaboration gives Chinese engineers access to global best practices while driving rapid local innovation.

According to McKinsey & Company (2024), Chinese automation companies have grown their robotics revenue by roughly twenty-five percent annually since 2018, driven by both export growth and domestic modernization.

The AI and Vision Layer

Behind China's robotics expansion lies a powerful AI and vision infrastructure. Firms such as SenseTime (0020.HK), Megvii, and Hikvision (002415.SZ) specialize in computer vision—the technology that allows robots to recognize objects, people, and environments.

Together, LiDAR and computer vision form the "eyes" of China's robot economy. Supported by domestic AI models, cloud networks, and government-backed R&D programs, they create an ecosystem that can design, manufacture, and deploy autonomous systems entirely within China's borders.

Robotics in Logistics and Urban Systems

China's booming e-commerce sector accelerated automation in logistics, delivery, and urban transport. Companies such as JD Logistics, Meituan, and Pudu Robotics deploy fleets of robots for warehouse management and last-mile delivery.

Autonomous vehicle developers like Neolix and WeRide test delivery shuttles and driverless taxis across Chinese cities. Robotics is also transforming agriculture, construction, and healthcare through automation of repetitive and hazardous tasks.

China's government encourages these transitions by pairing automation with retraining initiatives to mitigate job displacement.

Government Policy and Funding

The Chinese government drives robotics growth through national and local programs. The Ministry of Industry and Information Technology (MIIT) provides tax incentives and startup grants, while regional governments build technology parks in Shenzhen, Suzhou, and Hangzhou dedicated to robotics innovation.

These programs foster collaboration among universities, corporations, and research centers. The result is a dense network of innovation hubs producing global exporters as well as agile niche startups.

Invest AI Viewpoint

China represents the scale model of robotics expansion: rapid, state-backed, and vertically integrated. Its dominance in LiDAR and optical systems gives it strategic leverage in the global robotics supply chain.

While geopolitical risks and regulatory opacity pose challenges, China's ongoing investments in automation, AI, and semiconductor manufacturing ensure that it will remain indispensable to global production.

We believe investors should view Chinese robotics as a long-term industrial position rather than a short-term speculative play. Exposure to China means exposure to the world's largest and fastest-growing manufacturing ecosystem.

Investor Takeaways

- Track Chinese robotics leaders: Siasun Robot (300024.SZ), Estun Automation (002747.SZ), and EFORT Intelligent Equipment (688165.SS).
- Follow LiDAR specialists: Hesai Technology (HSAI), RoboSense (002813.SZ), and Innovusion.
- Watch AI and vision firms: SenseTime (0020.HK), Megvii, and Hikvision (002415.SZ).
- Study logistics robotics companies: JD Logistics, Meituan, and Pudu Robotics.
- Monitor ETFs with Chinese automation exposure: KBA, CQQQ, and MCHI.

# 14

# Europe: Safety, Ethics, and Integration Leadership: How the Continent Builds Robots with Conscience.

**Europe: Safety, Ethics, and Integration Leadership**

Europe builds robots with conscience. While Japan focuses on precision and China on scale, Europe leads through regulation, safety, and system integration. Its approach to robotics combines strong engineering with deep cultural concern for ethics, privacy, and labor impact.

**A Foundation of Engineering Excellence**

Europe's robotics industry was born inside factories. Germany, Switzerland, and Italy pioneered automation long before it was called robotics. Companies such as ABB (ABBN.SW), KUKA (KUKAY), and Siemens (SIE.DE) turned precision manufacturing into an art form.

Europe also championed the concept of collaborative robotics, or cobots; machines designed to work safely alongside people. Universal Robots, based in Denmark and owned by Teradyne, brought cobots into mainstream manufacturing. According to the International Federation of Robotics (2024), Europe remains the world's top market for collaborative robots, accounting for nearly half of global installations.

**Safety and Ethical Design**

Europe's commitment to ethics and safety sets it apart. The European Commission (2024) enforces strict rules for AI transparency, data privacy, and machine accountability through the Artificial Intelligence Act. The law requires companies to assess risks, disclose data use, and ensure human oversight.

These standards may slow deployment, but they increase trust. Investors and consumers know that European robots must meet some of the highest safety requirements on earth. In healthcare, manufacturing, and logistics, that reputation is a competitive edge.

European research centers also lead in human–machine interaction and safety design. The Fraunhofer Institutes in Germany, EPFL in Switzerland, and TU Delft in the Netherlands develop soft robotics, tactile sensors, and fail-safe systems for industrial and medical use.

**Integration over Disruption**

Europe's robotics strategy favors integration, not disruption. Instead of replacing workers, European robots assist them. This philosophy aligns with Europe's social and labor policies, using automation to enhance productivity while preserving craftsmanship and employment.

Siemens MindSphere, ABB Ability, and Dassault Systèmes 3DEXPERIENCE are leading examples of European digital integration. These platforms connect machines, software, and data into unified ecosystems that make manufacturing cleaner, safer, and more efficient (Siemens, 2024).

**The Green Robotics Movement**

Europe is linking robotics with sustainability. Automation reduces waste, improves energy efficiency, and supports recycling. The European Green Deal (European Commission, 2024) funds projects that use robotics for renewable energy, precision agriculture, and smart logistics.

Companies such as Schneider Electric (SU.PA) and Bosch Rexroth integrate robotics with energy management and resource optimization. This convergence of climate goals and industrial technology has created a new field; green robotics, where sustainability itself becomes a growth market.

**Regional Strengths**

- Germany: Industrial and automotive robotics (KUKA, Siemens, Bosch).
- Switzerland: High-precision automation and sensors (ABB, Stäubli).
- France: Design and digital twin software (Dassault Systèmes, Schneider Electric).
- Denmark: Collaborative robots (Universal Robots, Mobile Industrial Robots).
- Italy: Packaging, food, and fashion manufacturing robotics.

Europe's diversity is its advantage. Each region contributes a distinct strength to the continent's robotics ecosystem.

Invest AI Viewpoint

Europe's advantage is trust. Its engineers build robots that are safe, interoperable, and sustainable. While others race ahead for scale, Europe builds for longevity. Its leadership in ethical standards will shape how global robotics is regulated and adopted.

We believe Europe's focus on safety, integration, and sustainability makes it one of the most dependable long-term investment regions. In a world increasingly automated, trust and compliance will become the ultimate competitive advantages.

Investor Takeaways

- Watch industrial leaders: ABB (ABBN.SW), Siemens (SIE.DE), and KUKA (KUKAY).
- Track collaborative robotics innovators: Universal Robots and Mobile Industrial Robots.
- Follow sustainability-focused companies: Schneider Electric (SU.PA) and Bosch Rexroth.
- Study software and integration providers: Dassault Systèmes (DSY.PA) and Siemens MindSphere.
- Consider ETFs with European automation exposure: HEZU, FPEU, and BOTZ.

# 15

# Emerging Markets: India, South Korea, and ASEAN: The New Frontiers of Global Robotics and Automation

**Emerging Markets: India, South Korea, and ASEAN Automation Hubs**

Not every robotics breakthrough begins in Silicon Valley or Tokyo. Around the world, emerging markets are building their own centers of innovation, fast, flexible, and full of potential. Nations such as India, South Korea, Singapore, and Vietnam are turning automation into national strategy. Together they represent the next wave of global robotics growth.

**India: The Digital Manufacturing Frontier**

India's strength lies in software. Its large technology workforce, strong education base, and expanding AI sector make it a natural hub for robotics development.

Government programs such as Make in India and Digital India promote local manufacturing and industrial automation (Ministry of Commerce, India, 2024). Companies like Tata Elxsi (TATAELXSI.NS), HCL Technologies

(HCLTECH.NS), and Wipro (WIPRO.NS) integrate AI, IoT, and robotics into smart factories.

Startups including Systemantics, GreyOrange, and Addverb Technologies design warehouse and logistics robots that are now exported around the world. India's robotics growth is also powered by international investment from Japanese, American, and European partners.

According to Deloitte (2024), India's robotics and automation market is expected to exceed twenty-five billion U.S. dollars by 2030. Its combination of software talent, manufacturing capacity, and cost efficiency gives it a long-term advantage in global supply chains.

**South Korea: The Automation Innovator**

South Korea is one of the most automated nations in the world. Its robot density, measured as the number of robots per ten thousand manufacturing workers, ranks among the highest globally (International Federation of Robotics, 2024).

Domestic giants such as Hyundai (005380.KS), Samsung (005930.KS), and LG Electronics (066570.KQ) invest heavily in robotics, AI, and advanced manufacturing. Hyundai's 2021 acquisition of Boston Dynamics marked a decisive move into humanoid and logistics robotics (Hyundai Motor Group, 2024).

The Korean government views robotics as vital to economic resilience and demographic stability. As the workforce ages, robots are increasingly used in manufacturing, defense, healthcare, and retail. The Korea Institute for Robot Industry Advancement (KIRIA) supports collaboration between research centers and private companies to speed up innovation and commercialization.

Korean companies emphasize practical integration. Their robots are designed to fit seamlessly into existing industries rather than to disrupt them. This pragmatic approach has created steady growth and dependable investment opportunities.

**ASEAN: The Rising Automation Belt**

Across Southeast Asia, countries such as Singapore, Vietnam, Malaysia, and Thailand are becoming regional automation hubs. They combine manufacturing expertise with government incentives and strong foreign investment.

Singapore leads the region through its Smart Nation Initiative, which links robotics with sustainability and urban planning. The Advanced Remanufacturing and Technology Centre (ARTC) develops next-generation industrial robots in partnership with companies such as Siemens and Rolls-Royce (Singapore Economic Development Board, 2024).

Vietnam and Thailand are emerging as manufacturing alternatives to China. Global corporations are shifting production to these markets to diversify supply chains and reduce geopolitical risk. Robotics adoption in Southeast Asia is expanding quickly, especially in electronics, automotive, and logistics sectors.

**The Global Supply Chain Shift**

As global manufacturing realigns, emerging markets will supply both components and expertise. They offer flexibility, competitive costs, and expanding technical talent. For investors, these economies represent early-stage growth with enormous potential.

Regional trade frameworks such as the Regional Comprehensive Economic Partnership (RCEP) are accelerating the exchange of technology and capital between these nations. As they become more interconnected, robotics will emerge as a shared regional strength.

**Invest AI Viewpoint**

Emerging markets represent the true growth frontier for robotics. They may not lead in design or AI architecture, but they will dominate production and deployment.

India will supply the software and systems integration talent. South Korea will contribute advanced automation technology. ASEAN nations will provide the manufacturing base and large-scale deployment. Together these regions form a global value chain that balances innovation with scale.

We believe the next decade's robotics boom will be shaped by collaboration between developed and emerging markets. The future of robotics will not belong to one nation but to a connected network of regional ecosystems.

**Investor Takeaways**

- Track Indian automation and AI firms such as Tata Elxsi (TATAELXSI.NS), HCL Technologies (HCLTECH.NS), and Addverb Technologies.
- Watch South Korean industrial leaders such as Hyundai (005380.KS), Samsung (005930.KS), and LG Electronics (066570.KQ).
- Follow ASEAN robotics initiatives such as Singapore's ARTC programs and Vietnam's industrial automation growth.
- Study ETFs that focus on emerging-market technology exposure such as EEMA, EEMV, and GMF.

# 16

# Valuations and Ratios in the Age of Robots: How to Read the Numbers Behind AI, Automation, and Crypto Investing

## Valuations and Ratios in the Age of Robots

### *How to Read the Numbers Behind the Machine Economy*

Investing in robotics and AI is exciting, but excitement without understanding can be dangerous. Behind every headline about humanoids or quantum AI lies a balance sheet, a ratio, and a real-world valuation. The goal of this chapter is simple: to teach you how to read those numbers so you can see which technologies are truly building value.

In the age of intelligent machines, data drives everything. It drives robots, it drives markets, and it drives returns. Whether you trade stocks or crypto tokens linked to infrastructure projects, learning how to interpret valuation metrics is how you separate innovation from hype.

## *Why Valuation Matters*

Valuation is the foundation of investing. It tells you how much a company or token is worth compared to what it earns, builds, or contributes.

In robotics, valuation is often complicated. Many of these companies are young, fast-growing, and reinvesting profits into research and development instead of reporting high earnings. That makes traditional ratios such as price-to-earnings (P/E) less useful.

Instead, investors must rely on a combination of financial and innovation metrics that reveal how effectively a company turns ideas into scalable products. In short, valuation is not just about profit. It is about progress.

## *Key Ratios for Robotics and AI Companies*

**1. Price-to-Sales (P/S) Ratio**

This ratio compares a company's market value to its annual sales. It is useful for growth companies that have revenue but limited profit. A lower P/S can suggest undervaluation, while a very high P/S means investors expect major growth.

*Example:* In early 2025, industrial firms such as ABB and Siemens trade around a P/S of 3 to 4, while AI-driven companies such as NVIDIA can reach 20 or more (Morningstar, 2025).

**2. Research and Development (R&D) Intensity**

This shows how much a company spends on innovation relative to its revenue. It is calculated by dividing R&D spending by total sales. In robotics, an R&D intensity between ten and twenty percent usually signals a strong focus on innovation and long-term leadership.

**3. Gross Margin**

This ratio measures how much profit remains after production costs. Higher margins, often above forty percent, signal efficiency and proprietary technology. Software-focused robotics firms tend to have higher margins than hardware manufacturers because digital systems scale faster than physical products.

**4. Debt-to-Equity (D/E) Ratio**

Expansion requires capital, but too much debt can make growth risky. A D/E ratio below one generally indicates a healthy balance between borrowing and equity.

**5. Return on Invested Capital (ROIC)**

This shows how well management converts investment into profit. A high ROIC, typically above ten percent, signals strong leadership and efficient use of resources.

## *Why These Ratios Matter to You*

If you buy shares in a robotics company or hold tokens in a DePIN network, you are effectively betting on its ability to turn technology into cash flow. Ratios help you see the truth beneath marketing.

- A low P/S with rising R&D spending may suggest an undervalued innovator.
- A high D/E might warn of future funding problems.
- Strong ROIC and margin performance often point to durable companies that can survive downturns.

In the crypto world, these same ideas appear in different language. When you evaluate a blockchain or infrastructure token, you are still looking at capital efficiency, developer activity, and network growth—the same logic behind financial ratios, just expressed in decentralized form.

### *The Challenge of Emerging Sectors*

Valuing robotics and AI firms requires patience and context. Established industrial players such as FANUC and ABB generate steady revenue from long-term contracts. Younger companies, such as Figure AI or Apptronik, operate on potential rather than profit.

For these innovators, valuation depends on forward-looking projections; what analysts believe the market for humanoids, sensors, or LiDAR could become. Investors should compare companies within the same niche. A semiconductor supplier cannot be measured the same way as a simulation software firm. Each has its own financial rhythm and risk profile.

### *The ETF Shortcut*

For most investors, the simplest way to gain exposure is through **exchange-traded funds (ETFs)**. Funds such as **ROBO**, **BOTZ**, and **IRBO** include dozens of automation and AI companies. They blend mature manufacturers with emerging innovators, spreading both risk and opportunity.

According to Deloitte (2024), robotics and automation ETFs have grown more than sixty percent in assets since 2020, showing increasing investor confidence in the long-term sector. ETFs also remove the need to pick winners individually, giving exposure to the overall growth trend.

### *Forward Indicators: Reading the Hidden Signals*

Beyond ratios, there are subtle clues that reveal a company's momentum:

- **Patent filings** often predict new product lines.
- **Capital expenditures** (CapEx) show whether a company is expanding production or improving efficiency.
- **Hiring trends** in engineering and R&D departments suggest internal

innovation and growth capacity (McKinsey & Company, 2024).

In crypto and decentralized infrastructure projects, these same signals appear as rising developer activity, increasing node counts, and more partnerships. Together, they form a picture of innovation health.

### *Why This Matters in the Stock and Crypto Landscape*

Understanding valuation gives you discipline. In a world driven by hype, it keeps you grounded. When social media celebrates a new AI startup or a robot token surges overnight, ratios help you ask the right questions:

- Is this company creating sustainable value or chasing attention?
- Are they investing in innovation or spending on marketing?
- Is their balance sheet healthy enough to survive competition?

When you can answer these questions with real data, you move from speculator to investor.

### *Invest AI Viewpoint*

The robotics and AI economy rewards vision and discipline equally. Traditional valuation tools such as P/S and ROIC still matter, but investors must interpret them through the lens of innovation.

We believe the companies that win will be those that invest deeply in R&D, maintain healthy balance sheets, and show consistent operational efficiency. In crypto and DePIN ecosystems, the same principles apply: networks that reward real-world utility and build durable infrastructure will create lasting value.

Patience is the hidden superpower. The biggest returns in robotics and AI often appear years after the first wave of headlines. The future belongs to those who study the numbers, not just the news.

### *Investor Takeaways*

- Evaluate robotics and AI companies with a mix of traditional ratios and innovation metrics.
- Compare firms within their own sectors to ensure fair analysis.
- Track R&D intensity and ROIC as indicators of long-term health.
- Use ETFs such as ROBO, BOTZ, and IRBO for diversified exposure.
- Watch patent filings, hiring trends, and developer activity as early signals of innovation strength.

# 17

# R&D and Revenue Intensity: How to Spot the Next Breakthrough in Robotics, AI, and Tech Investing

**R&D and Revenue Intensity**

*How to Spot Innovation Before the Market Does*

Innovation is the lifeblood of robotics and artificial intelligence. Every movement a robot makes, every new chip that processes data faster, begins in a research lab. Investors who understand research and development, or R&D, often see the future before the market does.

**Why R&D Matters**

Robotics and AI companies depend on R&D more than almost any other sector. Their products evolve constantly. Hardware wears out, software updates monthly, and competition is relentless. Companies that keep investing in innovation move forward. Those that slow down quickly lose relevance.

R&D spending shows a company's belief in its own future. High R&D intensity, meaning a large percentage of revenue devoted to research, signals long-term ambition over short-term profit.

According to McKinsey & Company (2024), robotics firms that consistently reinvest more than ten percent of revenue into R&D outperform their peers in productivity and market value over five years.

How to Measure R&D Intensity

R&D intensity is calculated as:

**R&D Intensity = (R&D Expenditure ÷ Total Revenue) × 100**

The number shows how much of each dollar earned is reinvested in research.

- Mature industrial firms such as ABB or Siemens maintain R&D intensity between six and eight percent.
- AI and semiconductor developers such as NVIDIA or AMD often exceed twenty percent.
- Early-stage robotics startups may spend more than half of their revenue on development before reaching profitability.

Each group reflects a different stage of innovation. That is why investors should compare companies within the same niche rather than across the entire robotics ecosystem.

### The Link Between R&D and Revenue Growth

Consistent R&D investment often predicts future revenue expansion. When prototypes turn into products, the connection between innovation and sales becomes visible.

Companies with strong research pipelines tend to launch products faster and adapt better to market shifts. FANUC, for example, keeps refining its robotic arms through new sensors and software, maintaining dominance in industrial automation. NVIDIA's ongoing R&D focus on GPU architecture created entire industries around AI computing and simulation (NVIDIA, 2024).

### The Hidden Value of Patents

Patents are the receipts of innovation. Tracking patent filings helps investors see which firms are building new technology that others may eventually license.

The World Intellectual Property Organization (2024) lists Japan, the United States, and China as the top three nations for robotics-related patent activity. Within these countries, companies such as Toyota, Siemens, and ABB hold hundreds of patents tied to motion control, automation software, and machine safety.

Patent quantity matters less than influence. A smaller portfolio with many citations or cross-licensing deals can indicate deeper market impact.

### Balancing R&D and Profitability

Spending heavily on R&D only pays off when managed with discipline. Investors should study both R&D intensity and operating margin to see how well innovation is funded without creating instability.

High burn rates can mean creativity or chaos. The goal is to find firms where investment translates into real progress; new launches, market share gains, or strategic partnerships.

### R&D as a National and Economic Signal

At a global level, R&D spending reveals national priorities. The United States and Japan lead in AI and automation funding. China is rapidly expanding through state-supported manufacturing and logistics programs. Europe emphasizes safety and collaboration through its Horizon Europe research grants (European Commission, 2024).

Following national R&D budgets helps investors anticipate which countries and industries will produce the next wave of commercial breakthroughs before they reach stock exchanges.

Why It Matters in the Investment Landscape

In both traditional markets and crypto-based innovation networks, R&D intensity acts like a heartbeat. It shows where real building is happening. For robotics and DePIN investors, tracking these ratios helps identify which teams are inventing the next wave of technology rather than just marketing it.

In the same way that a blockchain's developer activity signals future strength, a robotics company's R&D investment reveals its staying power. High and consistent R&D spending is one of the clearest signs of conviction.

Invest AI Viewpoint

R&D intensity is the purest indicator of innovation momentum. It measures vision, resilience, and belief. In the robotics and AI economy, it is one of the earliest and most reliable predictors of future success.

We believe investors should value persistence over perfection. Innovation compounds like interest: the more consistent the investment, the greater the eventual return. Companies that keep building through downturns often emerge as category leaders when the market rebounds.

Investor Takeaways

- Track R&D intensity in company filings and annual reports.
- Compare R&D ratios within the same industry segments such as hardware, software, or sensors.
- Monitor patent filings, research partnerships, and government grants as early signals of innovation.
- Balance exposure between high-spending innovators such as NVIDIA or AMD and stable industrial leaders such as ABB or Siemens.
- Treat R&D spending as both a growth indicator and a measure of long-term resilience.

# 18

# ETF and Venture Signals: The Smart Investor's Guide to Robotics, AI, Quantum, and DePIN Opportunities

**ETF and Venture Signals: Top Future Forward Robotics, Artificial Intelligence, Quantum, and DePIN Investments**

## *How to Build Smart Exposure to the Machine Economy*

The robotics revolution is no longer theory. It has become an asset class. Exchange-traded funds, venture capital, and digital infrastructure networks are now the arteries through which automation capital flows. Investors today can build exposure across every layer of the machine economy, from industrial robots and AI software to decentralized networks that power autonomous systems.

## *The Rise of Robotics and AI ETFs*

Exchange-traded funds, or ETFs, are the most direct way for investors to participate in robotics, AI, and quantum computing without having to pick individual companies. Each fund holds dozens of stocks, offering diversification across software, semiconductors, logistics, and automation.

The global value of robotics and AI ETFs now exceeds thirty-five billion U.S. dollars (Morningstar, 2025). That growth reflects investor confidence that automation is not a trend but the foundation of the next industrial era.

**The Global X Robotics and Artificial Intelligence ETF (BOTZ)** remains one of the most popular funds. It includes **NVIDIA, ABB, Keyence, Intuitive Surgical, and Yaskawa**, all leaders in AI-driven automation. The **ROBO Global Robotics and Automation ETF (ROBO)** provides a balanced mix of manufacturers and service firms such as **Cognex, Rockwell Automation, and FANUC.**

Investors who prefer equal-weighted exposure often choose the **iShares Robotics and Artificial Intelligence ETF (IRBO)**, which holds **Alphabet, AMD, Amazon, Siemens, and Sony**. For higher-risk, innovation-driven exposure, **ARK Autonomous Technology and Robotics (ARKQ)** focuses on disruptive companies such as **Tesla, Trimble, and 3D Systems.**

Machine learning investors may explore the **WisdomTree Artificial Intelligence and Innovation ETF (WTAI)**, which includes **Palantir, C3.ai, and Snowflake**. For quantum exposure, the **Defiance Quantum ETF (QTUM)** features holdings such as **IBM, D-Wave, Honeywell, and NVIDIA** (Global X, 2025).

### *Quantum and Machine Learning Exposure*

Quantum computing and AI-focused ETFs provide access to the computing power that makes automation intelligent. The **VanEck Future of AI and Quantum ETF (AIQ)** includes major AI and quantum players such as **NVIDIA, IBM, IonQ, and Microsoft**.

Other funds connect robotics with blockchain and data infrastructure.

The **Amplify Transformational Data Sharing ETF (BLOK)** invests in companies like **Coinbase, IBM, and NVIDIA**, bridging digital networks and automation. The **Horizons Global Robotics ETF (HROB)** offers international exposure to **ABB, Siemens, FANUC, and Keyence.** For investors interested in smart infrastructure, the **SPDR Kensho Intelligent Structures ETF (SIMS)** includes **Honeywell, Autodesk, Trimble, and Schneider Electric.**

## *Venture Capital and Private Market Signals*

Venture capital remains the lifeblood of early robotics innovation. In 2024, robotics and AI startups raised over eighteen billion U.S. dollars globally (Crunchbase, 2025).

Key categories include humanoid robotics, warehouse automation, and AI-driven factory control. **Figure AI**, **Sanctuary AI**, and **Apptronik** are leading humanoid design, while **Rapid Robotics** and **Covariant** are redefining industrial automation. Simulation firms such as **Adept AI** and **Physical Intelligence** are advancing how robots learn virtually before entering the real world.

Top venture investors; **Sequoia Capital, Andreessen Horowitz, Tiger Global, and SoftBank Vision Fund;** have increased their robotics exposure. These firms are funding the private companies that will likely enter future ETFs within the next decade.

## *The DePIN and Crypto Infrastructure Frontier*

A new investment frontier has emerged: **DePIN**, or Decentralized Physical Infrastructure Networks. These blockchain-based systems reward physical devices such as sensors, drones, and servers for contributing real-world computing power, energy, or data to shared networks.

- **Render (RNDR)** pays GPU owners for distributed rendering tasks.
- **Akash (AKT)** allows companies to rent decentralized cloud computing.
- **Bittensor (TAO)** enables AI models to exchange data and computation for tokens.
- **Hivemapper** builds a decentralized map of the world through driver cameras.
- **Filecoin (FIL)** and **Arweave (AR)** provide decentralized storage.
- **IoTeX (IOTX)** secures device identity and communication (Messari, 2025).

These networks link robotics, AI, and blockchain by giving machines an economic system. In this model, devices not only work but also earn and trade resources autonomously.

### *Building a Modern Robotics Portfolio*

A modern robotics portfolio should balance stability with innovation. Long-term investors can anchor their holdings in diversified robotics ETFs such as **BOTZ, ROBO, and IRBO**, then add specialized AI and quantum funds like **QTUM, AIQ, and ARKQ**. Semiconductor ETFs such as **SOXX** or **SMH** provide exposure to the hardware behind the revolution.

For investors comfortable with frontier risk, a small allocation to **DePIN tokens** can add speculative upside linked to decentralized infrastructure. The goal is balance: steady growth from industrial and software equities combined with selective exposure to early-stage technologies that could multiply as automation expands.

### *The Venture Signal*

Venture activity often predicts where public markets are heading. Most companies that later appear in robotics and AI ETFs start as privately funded startups. Tracking major venture rounds gives investors an early view of future market leaders.

The firms building momentum today; **Figure AI**, **Sanctuary AI**, **Adept AI**, and **Covariant**; may become tomorrow's ETF holdings, just as **NVIDIA**, **ABB**, and **Intuitive Surgical** once did.

## *Invest AI Viewpoint*

ETFs and venture investments form the roadmap of innovation capital. They reveal where institutional money is flowing before mainstream investors notice. The most powerful opportunities exist at the intersection of robotics, AI, quantum computing, and decentralized infrastructure.

We believe investors who blend stable ETF exposure with selective positions in frontier assets will capture both the current wave of automation and the foundations of the intelligent machine economy that will define the decades ahead.

## *Investor Takeaways*

- Start with diversified robotics and AI ETFs such as BOTZ, ROBO, and IRBO.
- Add specialized AI and quantum exposure through QTUM, AIQ, and ARKQ.
- Balance growth with stability using semiconductor ETFs such as SOXX and SMH.
- Track venture-backed innovators such as Figure AI, Sanctuary AI, and Covariant for future IPO potential.
- Follow DePIN projects such as Render, Akash, and Bittensor for long-term exposure to decentralized AI infrastructure.

## *Final Recap: Key ETFs, Stocks, and Crypto Assets Mentioned*

**Major Robotics and AI ETFs:** BOTZ, ROBO, IRBO, ARKQ, WTAI, QTUM, RBOT, DRIV, AIQ, BLOK, HROB, SIMS

**Quantum and Semiconductor ETFs:** AIQ, QTUM, SOXX, SMH

**Public Robotics and Automation Stocks:** NVIDIA, ABB, Keyence, Intuitive Surgical, Yaskawa, Cognex, Rockwell Automation, FANUC, Alphabet, AMD, Amazon, Siemens, Sony, Tesla, Trimble, 3D Systems, Palantir, C3.ai, Snowflake, IBM, D-Wave, Honeywell, Microsoft, Coinbase, Autodesk, Schneider Electric

**Private or Venture Robotics Firms:** Figure AI, Sanctuary AI, Apptronik, Rapid Robotics, Covariant, Adept AI, Physical Intelligence

**Crypto and DePIN Infrastructure Tokens:** Render (RNDR), Akash (AKT), Bittensor (TAO), Hivemapper, Filecoin (FIL), Arweave (AR), IoTeX (IOTX)

# 19

# Investor Playbooks: Building Wealth in the Age of Robotics, AI, Quantum, and Machine Economies

**How to Invest Intelligently in the New Industrial Revolution**

The robotics revolution is no longer theoretical. It is here, and it demands a new kind of investor who understands that technology cycles now move faster than economic cycles. The Investor Playbook is your guide for navigating this transformation with clarity, confidence, and discipline.

The Purpose of the Playbook

Investing in robotics and AI is not about chasing hype. It is about building intelligent exposure. These industries evolve quickly, and the winners of tomorrow may still be private startups or component suppliers that few investors notice today. The goal is to create a repeatable system for identifying, tracking, and holding innovation.

A strong playbook balances two forces:

Core conviction, meaning holdings that preserve value through market cycles, and adaptive intelligence, meaning the flexibility to pivot when technology or economic conditions change.

The Three Pillars of Smart Robotics Investing

1. The Core Foundation

This is the long-term anchor of your portfolio. It includes diversified ETFs, established industrial leaders, and major semiconductor firms. These holdings provide steady growth and, in many cases, reliable dividends.

Core examples include ETFs such as BOTZ, ROBO, and IRBO, industrial names like ABB, Siemens, and Rockwell, and semiconductor innovators such as NVIDIA, AMD, and Intel.

2. The Growth Frontier

This layer targets companies driving the next wave of disruption, including humanoid robotics, AI software, simulation systems, and decentralized infrastructure. These assets carry higher volatility but also greater upside potential.

Firms such as Figure AI, Sanctuary AI, and Apptronik in humanoids, or Render, Akash, and Bittensor in decentralized infrastructure, belong in this group. A moderate twenty-percent allocation captures the frontier while maintaining portfolio stability.

3. The Opportunity Layer

This is where tactical investing happens. It includes early IPOs, emerging-market automation firms, and thematic funds such as QTUM for quantum computing or WTAI for machine learning. Positions in this category can change as new technologies mature. Investors who monitor venture funding, government initiatives, and adoption cycles gain early access to the next wave of growth.

- The 70–20–10 Framework
- A clear structure for long-term balance:
- Seventy percent in core robotics and AI ETFs or blue-chip automation stocks.
- Twenty percent in high-growth innovation and frontier assets.
- Ten percent in speculative exposure such as early-stage cryptos, DePIN tokens, or new IPOs.

This mix allows consistent performance while keeping your portfolio connected to innovation.

**Timing and Discipline**

Investing in emerging technology requires patience and clear rules. The best investors treat robotics as infrastructure rather than entertainment. The industry moves in overlapping five- to seven-year cycles. Each new wave, such as AI, quantum computing, or humanoid systems, builds upon the last.

Focus on accumulation instead of perfect timing. Add during pullbacks, hold through volatility, and review your core holdings each quarter. Emotional trading damages long-term results. The automation era rewards consistency and commitment.

**Behavioral Rules for the Machine Economy**

Study before buying. Understand what the company builds and how it earns.

Follow capital, not hype. Venture rounds and R&D spending reveal more than social media trends.

**Diversify across intelligence types, combining industrial automation, AI software, and digital infrastructure.**

Stay liquid enough to adjust when new opportunities appear.

Think globally. Robotics leadership spans Japan, China, Europe, and emerging markets.

**Early Warning and Signal Monitoring**

The best investors track early signals of growth. These include patent filings, venture rounds, acquisitions, and ETF rebalancing activity.

When a fund such as BOTZ or ARKQ adds a new company, it often reflects institutional confidence before retail investors notice. Government programs that fund automation or semiconductor expansion can also move regional markets, so staying alert to policy updates is essential.

**Integrating Crypto and DePIN into a Robotics Portfolio**

**DePIN** assets form the economic framework of the machine economy. They allow devices to earn, share data, and transact automatically. While speculative, they can complement traditional holdings.

Leading examples include Render (RNDR) for GPU sharing, Akash (AKT) for decentralized cloud computing, and Bittensor (TAO) for tokenized AI collaboration. As digital infrastructure and regulation evolve, these projects could support future robotics networks by enabling decentralized computing and data exchange.

**Case Study: The Patient Accumulator**

Consider an investor who began accumulating BOTZ, NVIDIA, and ABB during the 2022 downturn. By 2025, those holdings had compounded through exposure to AI hardware, industrial robotics, and automation ETFs. Instead of chasing trends, that investor quietly built long-term positions and allowed innovation to compound naturally.

**The Macro Connection**

The robotics and AI economy is expanding faster than overall global GDP. McKinsey & Company (2024) estimates that generative AI and automation together could contribute between 2.6 and 4.4 trillion U.S. dollars in annual value across global industries. PwC (2023) projects that AI could add up to 15.7 trillion U.S. dollars to global GDP by 2030. Aligning a portfolio with this megatrend means owning a share of the next industrial base.

Invest AI Viewpoint

The winning strategy in the robotics era combines conviction, curiosity, and caution. Conviction keeps investors grounded during volatility. Curiosity identifies new opportunities. Caution maintains discipline and protects capital.

Robotics and AI will reshape every major industry just as the internet transformed communication. The difference now is that machines will not only compute but also act, learn, and build. Those who own the systems behind them will hold equity in the next industrial age.

Investor Takeaways

Use the 70-20-10 framework to balance core, frontier, and speculative exposure.

- Combine robotics ETFs such as BOTZ, ROBO, and IRBO with AI and quantum funds such as QTUM, AIQ, and WTAI.
- Track R&D spending, venture rounds, and ETF rebalances for early signals of innovation.
- Treat DePIN tokens such as Render, Akash, and Bittensor as long-term

strategic experiments.

- Stay patient, diversified, and globally focused. Consistency and time remain the most powerful tools in the age of automation.

# 20

# Policy, Labor, and Ethics: Navigating Regulation and Human Impact in the Robotics Economy

Every industrial revolution changes society, but the robotics age is rewriting the relationship between humans, machines, and institutions. Policy, labor, and ethics are now as central to investment decisions as innovation and valuation.

**The Policy Landscape**

Governments around the world are racing to define the rules for robotics and artificial intelligence. These policies influence which companies succeed, which technologies get funding, and how global trade adapts to automation.

In the United States, federal initiatives under the CHIPS and Science Act and National AI Strategy provide billions in funding for semiconductor manufacturing, AI research, and automation infrastructure (U.S. Department of Commerce, 2024). These programs strengthen domestic production and create opportunities for companies in robotics hardware and software.

In the European Union, the Artificial Intelligence Act (AIA) establishes the world's most comprehensive regulatory framework for AI safety, privacy, and accountability (European Commission, 2024). It categorizes AI systems by risk level and requires transparency and human oversight. Robotics firms operating in Europe must design for compliance, giving European companies a long-term trust advantage.

In Asia, Japan's Society 5.0 initiative integrates robotics, AI, and IoT into a human-centered model of development. China's Made in China 2025 policy continues to push large-scale automation, while South Korea and Singapore offer tax incentives for smart manufacturing. Policy is not an afterthought; it is now the hidden infrastructure of global innovation.

**The Labor Shift**

Automation often sparks fear of job loss, but the data paints a more complex picture. According to McKinsey & Company (2024), while automation will displace up to fifteen percent of global labor by 2035, it could also create up to twelve million new roles in robotics maintenance, AI engineering, and system management.

In advanced economies, the focus is shifting from replacement to reskilling. Governments and corporations are investing in programs that teach digital literacy, robotics operation, and AI integration. Workers are learning to collaborate with machines rather than compete against them.

In developing nations, robotics can raise productivity and wages by modernizing agriculture, logistics, and manufacturing. The balance between disruption and opportunity depends on how fast education systems and industry training evolve.

**The Ethics of Intelligent Machines**

Ethics sits at the heart of robotics adoption. As machines take on more decision-making power, society must decide what boundaries exist. Ethical frameworks now guide everything from humanoid assistance to autonomous vehicles.

Europe's AI Act leads in codifying transparency and accountability. In the United States, the White House Office of Science and Technology Policy (OSTP) introduced the Blueprint for an AI Bill of Rights (2023) to protect individuals from bias and misuse of AI. Japan's Ministry of Economy, Trade, and Industry promotes "Human-Centric AI" principles to ensure technology aligns with social harmony.

The ethical debate extends into robotics research itself. Questions about bias in AI models, algorithmic control, and human dignity are shaping public perception. For investors, ethical design and compliance reduce long-term risk. Companies that follow clear ethical standards often gain better access to funding and partnerships.

**Global Standards and Certification**

The International Organization for Standardization (ISO) has issued global standards for robot safety, including ISO 10218 for industrial robots and ISO/TS 15066 for collaborative robots. Compliance with these standards is now a major selling point.

This certification culture helps investors identify mature, globally ready firms. Companies that achieve ISO compliance are more likely to succeed in cross-border manufacturing and partnerships.

**Policy as an Investment Driver**

Investors often overlook regulation, but it determines entire industries. Subsidies for semiconductor production, for example, can boost companies like Intel, TSMC, and STMicroelectronics. Likewise, public investments in automation and AI research drive growth for industrial players such as ABB, Siemens, and FANUC.

Policy also affects risk. Trade disputes, export restrictions on chips, and privacy laws can shift competitive advantage. Monitoring policy announcements, funding bills, and international partnerships helps investors anticipate how the global robotics map will evolve.

**Social Sustainability and Corporate Governance**

Environmental, social, and governance (ESG) investing now includes robotics and AI. Automation reduces waste and energy use, but it also raises questions about workforce inclusion and data ethics.

Leading corporations address these through "ethical robotics charters" and sustainability reports. Companies that link robotics to human benefit; healthcare, accessibility, and clean energy; often earn public trust and investor loyalty.

**Invest AI Viewpoint**

Policy and ethics are not barriers; they are the blueprint for sustainable innovation. The next decade will favor companies that build responsibly, comply globally, and align automation with human values.

We believe that investors who understand the intersection of regulation and innovation will see clearer long-term returns. The future belongs to those who invest not only in intelligence but also in integrity.

**Investor Takeaways**

- Track national policies: U.S. CHIPS Act, EU AI Act, Japan's Society 5.0, and China's Made in China 2025.

- Monitor ESG metrics in robotics companies for long-term stability.
- Favor firms that disclose AI transparency, ethics, and compliance frameworks.
- Watch for ISO-certified robotics and AI systems to gauge maturity and export potential.
- Consider diversification across regions to balance regulatory and political risk.

# 21

# The Convergence: How Robotics, Quantum Computing, and Bio-Intelligence Are Fusing Into One Global System

**The Birth of a Unified Intelligence Infrastructure**

Every major technology eventually connects with another. The next era of progress will not come from isolated breakthroughs but from the meeting of once-separate fields. Artificial intelligence, robotics, quantum computing, and biology are beginning to merge into one global system of intelligence.

This marks a turning point. Machines will no longer just process information; they will begin to process reality itself.

**The End of Separation**

For decades, robotics focused on motion, AI on reasoning, and quantum computing on raw power. Each field advanced on its own path. Now they are converging. Faster chips, larger data flows, and shared cloud systems are bringing them together into a single framework of discovery.

AI models now rely on quantum optimization to train faster and solve complex problems. Robotics is borrowing ideas from biology, using living materials that move and repair themselves. Cloud platforms combine data from satellites, sensors, and biology to model the world in ways that were once impossible.

According to the World Economic Forum (2025), the fusion of AI, robotics, and biotechnology could add more than twenty trillion U.S. dollars to the global economy by 2040. It is changing the very meaning of a technology company.

**Quantum Intelligence and Robotics**

Quantum computing brings a new kind of power. A classical computer can simulate a few outcomes at a time. A quantum computer can explore millions. Applied to robotics, this ability allows machines to learn faster, adapt more effectively, and design better solutions.

Research from IBM Quantum and IonQ shows that quantum algorithms can improve motion planning, energy efficiency, and materials design for robots (IBM Research, 2025). In the future, robots will not need endless trial and error. They will learn by exploring thousands of possibilities in seconds.

Quantum sensing adds another layer of precision. These instruments measure gravity, magnetism, and acceleration so accurately that they could revolutionize navigation, geology, and medical imaging.

**Biohybrid Systems and Living Machines**

Robotics is starting to borrow from nature. Scientists at the University of Tokyo and MIT are developing hybrid machines made of living muscle tissue attached to synthetic structures. These robots move naturally, use biological energy, and can repair themselves after damage.

Another breakthrough is organoid intelligence, where living clusters of brain cells perform simple computing tasks. Studies from the Johns Hopkins Applied Physics Laboratory (2024) show that these "mini-brains" can recognize patterns more efficiently than traditional chips.

This points to a future where intelligence is not only mechanical or digital. It can also be living, adaptive, and self-healing.

**The Rise of the Machine Economy**

As robots become more capable and AI grows more autonomous, machines are beginning to join the economy. With the rise of DePIN and blockchain-based computing, devices can exchange energy, data, and payment directly.

This is the early stage of what many call the machine economy—a network of autonomous systems that trade and cooperate in real time.

Projects such as Render (RNDR), Akash (AKT), and Bittensor (TAO) are early examples. They reward contributors who share computing power or AI models (Messari, 2025). Over time, this new infrastructure could support global manufacturing, logistics, and smart cities.

**The Biological Merge**

Convergence is also reshaping the human body. Brain-computer interfaces, wearable robotics, and neural implants are helping people recover movement, improve cognition, and interact directly with machines.

Companies such as Neuralink, Synchron, and Paradromics are testing implants that translate brain activity into digital commands. These technologies may one day allow people to control robotic limbs or communicate directly with artificial intelligence.

As this relationship deepens, machines stop being simple tools. They become extensions of human ability.

## Investment Implications

Convergence is transforming every market. Semiconductor companies now work alongside quantum startups. Biotech labs partner with AI developers. Industrial manufacturers collaborate with neuroscience and cloud computing firms.

Investors can no longer think in narrow categories. The winners of the coming decades will be the ones that integrate different kinds of intelligence—companies that combine computing, movement, and biology.

For example, NVIDIA may extend its AI hardware dominance into biological simulation. IBM could connect quantum computing to medical research. Startups working on biohybrid robotics may grow into the next generation of industrial leaders.

## Invest AI Viewpoint

The next phase of progress will be driven by integration. The walls between biology, computing, and automation are disappearing. The goal is no longer to build faster chips or smarter algorithms but to create connected systems that unite the digital, physical, and biological worlds.

The most successful investors will not chase isolated trends. They will look for the places where technologies intersect and strengthen one another. Convergence is not a single moment in time. It is the long-term design of the future.

## Investor Takeaways

- Watch for partnerships that link AI, robotics, quantum computing, and biotechnology.
- Study advances in organoid intelligence, biohybrid materials, and neural engineering.
- Follow quantum computing companies such as IBM, IonQ, and Rigetti as they expand into AI optimization.
- Track decentralized computing networks like Render, Akash, and Bittensor that support machine-to-machine systems.
- Look for funds or ETFs that blend biotechnology, AI, and quantum innovation into one portfolio.

# 22

# Self-Driving Labs and AI Science Factories: How Autonomous Research Will Accelerate the Next Technological Revolution

**Inside the New Era of Automated Discovery, Quantum Acceleration, and the Business of Research as a Service**

*Self-Driving Labs and AI Science Factories*

How Autonomous Research Will Accelerate the Next Technological Revolution

Science is learning to think for itself. Around the world, laboratories are changing from manual workshops into intelligent systems powered by algorithms, robots, and quantum models. These self-driving labs mark the next great leap in automation and are transforming the speed of discovery.

From Manual Discovery to Automated Intelligence

Traditional research depends on repetition. Scientists design an experiment, run it, record results, and adjust the variables. A self-driving lab replaces that cycle with automation. Robots mix materials, sensors record data, and

AI models decide what to test next.

The goal is simple: shorten the path between idea and discovery. What once took months can now take hours. According to Nature (2024), autonomous laboratories can run nearly one hundred times more experiments per day than human teams.

This acceleration is already producing advances in materials, clean energy, medicine, and electronics.

**The Infrastructure of the AI Lab**

A self-driving laboratory runs on five essential systems:

1. Robotic automation for handling precision tasks such as pipetting, assembly, or chemical synthesis.
2. AI algorithms that analyze data and predict which combinations are most promising.
3. High-throughput sensors that collect continuous real-time measurements.
4. Cloud and quantum computing platforms for simulation and optimization.
5. Feedback networks that let the machines learn directly from results.

The University of Liverpool's Materials Acceleration Platform and Carnegie Mellon's A-Lab are leading examples. Both use robotics and machine learning to discover new catalysts and energy materials (Carnegie Mellon University, 2024).

**AI Science Factories**

Beyond individual labs, large-scale "AI science factories" are emerging. These facilities operate like manufacturing plants, but instead of producing goods, they produce discoveries.

Google DeepMind's GNoME Project uses AI to predict stable crystal structures. IBM Research applies Quantum-Accelerated Materials Simulation to identify new superconductors. Moderna and BioNTech combine robotics and machine learning to test mRNA therapies faster than ever before (IBM Research, 2025).

These science factories do not replace scientists; they extend them. Humans set the goals, while machines explore the possibilities. Together they form a continuous loop of invention.

**Quantum Discovery Engines**

Quantum computing is giving autonomous labs an even greater advantage. By modeling molecules at the atomic level, quantum processors can test thousands of reactions simultaneously. IonQ and Rigetti are already partnering with chemical and pharmaceutical firms to accelerate research pipelines.

Quantum sensors add extreme precision, measuring temperature, pressure, and magnetic resonance with unprecedented accuracy. This data allows AI systems to make better predictions and reduce experimental error.

**Economic and Investment Implications**

Automated research could reduce development costs in materials and pharmaceuticals by as much as eighty percent (McKinsey & Company, 2024). That efficiency will change how industries approach innovation.

Instead of funding long, uncertain research projects, companies can build modular AI labs that improve themselves over time. Governments are also taking notice. The U.S. Department of Energy and the European Union have launched "AI for Science" initiatives to integrate robotics and computation into public research.

For investors, this signals the rise of a new business model: Research as a Service (RaaS). Companies that build and rent automated discovery platforms will supply pharmaceutical, energy, and electronics industries with subscription-based innovation.

### Leading Companies and Startups

Major players include DeepMind, IBM Research, Sandia National Laboratories, BASF, and Schrödinger Inc. Startups such as LabGenius, Zymergen, Emerald Cloud Lab, and Chemify are already commercializing autonomous research.

In Asia, Japan's RIKEN Institute and China's Tsinghua AI Lab are constructing fully automated systems for material science and nanotechnology. Their findings will feed global supply chains for batteries, semiconductors, and sustainable materials.

### The Human Role

Automation raises an important question: what is left for humans to do? The answer is creativity and direction. Machines can test millions of possibilities, but only people can decide which questions matter.

The future of research belongs to collaboration between human imagination and machine precision. Automation will not replace scientists; it will multiply their reach and speed.

### Invest AI Viewpoint

Self-driving labs are no longer science fiction. They are the new foundation of discovery. In the coming decade, industries from healthcare to clean energy will adopt automated research as a standard.

Investors should look for companies that combine robotics, data infrastructure, and scientific intelligence. The future economy will belong to those who automate invention itself.

**Investor Takeaways**

- Watch companies leading AI-driven research such as DeepMind, IBM Research, Schrödinger, and BASF.
- Follow startups LabGenius, Chemify, and Emerald Cloud Lab that offer automated discovery platforms.
- Track national programs supporting AI-based science initiatives.
- Look for collaborations between quantum computing firms and chemical or biotech corporations.
- Recognize Research as a Service as a new investment category with long-term potential.

# 23

# Organoid Intelligence and Wetware Computing: How Living Cells Are Redefining the Future of AI and Robotics

## The Rise of Living Machines

The next revolution in computing may not be built; it may be grown.

While AI learns and robots move, a new form of intelligence is quietly taking shape in laboratories: biological computers made from living cells. Known as organoid intelligence, this field uses clusters of brain tissue grown from human stem cells to perform computation.

It sounds surreal, yet it is grounded in real science. And it could redefine what intelligence and technology mean in the coming decades.

## From Silicon Chips to Living Networks

For seventy years, computing has advanced through smaller transistors and faster circuits. But the limits of silicon are near. As components approach atomic scales, energy loss and heat become major barriers to progress.

Biology offers another path. The human brain performs roughly one exaflop of processing power while consuming about twenty watts of energy—the same as a light bulb. No man-made computer approaches that level of efficiency.

Researchers at Johns Hopkins University and the University of California, San Diego are leading organoid computing projects that grow three-dimensional clusters of neurons capable of forming miniature circuits. These "mini-brains" can already play simple video games like Pong and recognize visual patterns without traditional programming (Johns Hopkins Applied Physics Lab, 2024).

**How Organoid Computing Works**

Organoid computers function through living neural activity. Each neuron connects with thousands of others through electrical and chemical signals. Scientists attach electrodes and AI interfaces to record, train, and interpret this activity.

Over time, these neural clusters reorganize themselves to perform better, much like a human brain learning a new skill. Machine learning algorithms interpret this biological data and adjust inputs, creating a feedback loop between living tissue and digital systems.

This hybrid model is called wetware—the biological counterpart to hardware and software. It uses living cells as processors and communication nodes.

**The Promise of Organoid Intelligence**

Organoid intelligence offers several advantages:

- Energy efficiency. Biological neurons process information with extremely low power compared to data centers.
- Adaptability. Living neural tissue can rewire itself, giving it flexibility that no silicon chip can match.
- Long-term learning. Biological memory is stored chemically and structurally, allowing for lasting retention of learned behaviors.

According to Frontiers in Science (2024), early organoid systems already outperform classical computers in pattern recognition and adaptive learning tasks.

**Ethical and Practical Challenges**

Using human-derived neurons raises difficult ethical questions. Where does computation end and consciousness begin? Research centers maintain oversight by bioethics committees to ensure experiments do not cross boundaries of sentience or moral risk.

Practical challenges also remain. Organoids are fragile and must be sustained in nutrient solutions. They currently survive only for months. Scientists are experimenting with bio-scaffolds and hybrid chips to improve their stability.

Companies such as FinalSpark, Cortical Labs, and Koniku are pioneering efforts to commercialize wetware systems by linking living neurons to AI and robotics.

**Integration with Robotics and AI**

Imagine a humanoid robot that learns movement and balance through a biological feedback loop instead of digital code. That concept is already in progress. Researchers at TU Dresden and Harvard's Wyss Institute are developing "bio-sensing robots" that integrate living neurons for motion learning.

Wetware systems can also complement digital AI networks. Rather than replacing machine learning, they may train or refine it. In the future, biological processors could guide digital models through real-time adaptability, creating a continuous loop between organic and artificial intelligence.

**Investment and Research Opportunities**

Organoid intelligence remains an emerging field, but early investment opportunities are appearing. Biotechnology and neurotechnology companies focused on cell growth, neural mapping, and AI-driven neuroscience will form its foundation.

Promising sectors include:

- Biocomputing firms: FinalSpark, Cortical Labs, and Koniku.
- AI–neuroscience integrators: NVIDIA (AI hardware for neural data), Neuralink, and Synchron.
- Pharmaceutical and neurotechnology partners: Roche, Bayer, and Biogen.
- Academic and government collaborations: Johns Hopkins University, Harvard Wyss Institute, and the European Human Brain Project.

According to Deloitte (2025), hybrid biological computing could grow into a multi-trillion-dollar global market by 2050 if progress continues in scalability and energy efficiency.

**The Philosophy of Living Computation**

For centuries, humanity built machines to imitate life. Now, science is beginning to build machines from life. The implications are profound.

As living computers become more advanced, the boundaries between biological and artificial intelligence will blur. This transformation invites deep reflection: when intelligence grows naturally rather than mechanically, does technology return to nature; or transcend it altogether?

**Invest AI Viewpoint**

Organoid intelligence and wetware computing mark the dawn of living technology. These systems merge life with code, biology with computation.

For investors, this field is about vision rather than speed. It will take time to mature, but the companies that lead this convergence will shape the next computing era beyond quantum.

The future belongs to machines that think, adapt, and heal like living organisms. Investors who recognize this early will hold a stake in the biological evolution of intelligence.

**Investor Takeaways**

- Follow early biocomputing startups such as FinalSpark, Cortical Labs, and Koniku.
- Watch established firms including NVIDIA, Neuralink, and Biogen as they enter hybrid intelligence research.
- Track organoid intelligence studies from Johns Hopkins, UC San Diego, and the European Human Brain Project.
- Understand bioethics and regulation as essential growth drivers in this field.
- Prepare for a convergence of computing, biology, and robotics that will form a new innovation market.

# 24

# Organoid Intelligence, Safely Built: A High-Level Blueprint for Ethical Bio-Computing with Accredited Partners (Bonus)

**Author's Note on Ethical Innovation**

*This chapter presents a theoretical framework for the safe development of organoid intelligence and living technology.*

*It is not a laboratory manual, nor a guide for biological experimentation. The concepts described here are intended to inspire dialogue, ethics-first innovation, and collaborative research within accredited scientific institutions.*

*The ideas draw on current public research from organizations such as Johns Hopkins University, UC San Diego, and other pioneers in organoid computing. By expanding that work into a responsible "blueprint," Invest-AI encourages readers to imagine how future technologies might evolve when guided by transparency, safety, and respect for life itself.*

*This is an experimental thought exercise, part of the Invest-AI vision for future-forward, ethical investing and discovery.*

*If even one reader takes these ideas and transforms them; safely, legally, and compassionately, into real progress, the purpose of this book will have been fulfilled.*

**Organoid Intelligence: A High-Level Blueprint for a Responsible Pilot**

**1) Purpose, scope, and guardrails**

- Define the research question in plain language. Example: "Can a biological learning module improve adaptive control in simulated robotics tasks."
- Commit to ethics first. Require IRB or equivalent ethics board review, institutional biosafety oversight, and documented informed consent for any human-derived material handled by accredited partners.
- Set red lines. No attempts at consciousness assessment, no sensory deprivation paradigms, no long-term culture without continual ethics review.

**2) Partner model rather than DIY wet-lab**

- Work only with accredited universities, contract research organizations, or GMP-compliant biobanks that already culture brain organoids under oversight.
- Your team focuses on the software, data, simulation, and interface research questions. Your wet-lab partner handles all biological work inside approved facilities.

**3) System architecture at a glance**

- Biological module: partner-provided neural organoid within approved culture and recording hardware in their facility.
- Interface module: multi-electrode array or optical readout owned and managed by the partner. Your team receives processed, anonymized signals through secure APIs.
- Compute module: your cloud stack for preprocessing, feature extraction, and learning algorithms.
- Simulation module: physics sandbox for training tasks, robotics environments, or control challenges that feed back as stimuli.
- Governance module: automated logging, audit trails, experiment registration, and ethics checkpoints before any parameter change.

**4) Data and AI stack**

- Ingestion: receive de-identified signal features from the partner's recording system. No raw donor data or PHI.
- Representation: build embeddings of neural activity patterns and environmental states.
- Learning loop: reinforcement learning or active learning that proposes the next safe stimulus pattern to test, then waits for partner approval and delivery.
- Interpretability: time-frequency analysis, causal inference, and simple surrogate models to explain what patterns correlate with performance changes.
- Safety layer: rate limits on stimulus intensity, frequency, and duration as defined by the partner's ethics protocol.

**5) Task design without direct stimulation detailS**

- Start in software-only simulations that mirror what a biological module could improve, such as adaptive control or anomaly detection.
- Define performance metrics that are ethical and non-invasive. Focus

on classification accuracy, stability over time, and adaptability to distribution shifts.

- Pre-register evaluation plans so success and failure are measured consistently.

**6) Human-in-the-loop oversight**

- Require a human approver at the partner lab to review any AI-recommended condition changes before they are scheduled.
- Build dashboards that explain recommendations in plain language, including expected benefit, uncertainty, and safety envelope.
- Log every action with time stamps and rationale for later audits.

**7) Security, privacy, and provenance**

- Use segregated networks, access control, and cryptographic signing of data packets from the partner facility.
- Maintain provenance for every dataset and model checkpoint.
- Prohibit model training on any data that has not passed ethics and legal review.

**8) Risk register and red-team tests**

- List foreseeable risks: misuse of data, incorrect stimulation proposals, model hallucinations in analysis.
- Run tabletop exercises to simulate failures and verify that circuit-breakers work. Examples include automatic shutdown on anomalous activity or deviation from approved ranges.

**9) Documentation and reproducibility**

- Treat your project like a regulated software product. Maintain specs, versioned protocols, and change logs.

- Publish only high-level findings that do not contain operational lab details. Preprint ethics statement first, results second.

**10) Funding and partnership roadmap**

- Stage 1: simulation-only proofs of concept with public benchmarks and synthetic neural data.
- Stage 2: data-sharing agreement with an accredited lab for de-identified, partner-curated datasets.
- Stage 3: co-authored studies that evaluate whether biological signals improve specific tasks compared with silicon baselines.
- Stage 4: explore commercial paths like analytics, tooling, or "biological signal services" provided by accredited partners, not direct culturing.

## Skills and roles to recruit

- Ethics and compliance lead who understands IRB, biosafety, and data protection.
- Neurodata scientist experienced in spike train analysis, time-series modeling, and interpretability.
- ML engineer for reinforcement learning, uncertainty estimation, and active learning.
- Safety engineer for constraints, monitoring, and circuit-breakers.
- Security architect for data provenance and access control.
- Partnership manager to coordinate with the accredited wet-lab team.

## Milestones that respect safety

- Milestone A: publish the simulation-only pipeline, metrics, and governance spec.
- Milestone B: run retrospective studies on de-identified neural datasets supplied by partners.
- Milestone C: co-author a methods paper on safe recommendation

systems for human-reviewed stimulation planning, with no lab how-to.
- Milestone D: comparative study that shows whether the partner's biological signals improve a defined task over a silicon-only control.

**Practical alternatives for builders today**

If you want to contribute right now without touching biology:

- Build open simulation environments and benchmarks for "biological-in-the-loop" learning. Keep them modular and easy to reproduce.
- Create visualization and interpretability tools for neural-like time-series that help ethics boards and scientists understand model behavior.
- Work on governance tech: experiment registries, audit logs, and transparent recommendation dashboards.
- Sponsor or collaborate with accredited labs through formal agreements that keep all wet-lab work inside regulated facilities.

The future of organoid intelligence should be responsible by design. Focus on the software architecture, the safety rails, and the partnerships. Leave any culturing, handling, or stimulation procedures to accredited labs operating under formal oversight.

# 25

# Quantum Sensing and Networks: How Machines Will Perceive, Communicate, and Secure the Future

**The Next Leap in Perception, Security, and Intelligence**

*Inside the New Infrastructure of Perception, Encryption, and Global Intelligence*

Robots today can see, hear, and process information, but soon they will sense reality in ways humans cannot. The next decade will bring machines equipped with quantum sensors that measure gravity, time, and magnetic fields with unprecedented precision.

These tools are no longer science fiction. They already exist in research labs and early commercial trials. Together with quantum networks that transmit information through entanglement, they will reshape how data, motion, and intelligence move across the world.

**What Is Quantum Sensing?**

Quantum sensing uses the properties of subatomic particles; such as spin, coherence, and entanglement to detect extremely small physical changes. Unlike traditional sensors that rely on mechanical or optical feedback, quantum sensors react to the quantum state of matter itself.

They can detect variations once thought undetectable: gravitational shifts beneath the Earth's surface, magnetic fields from individual neurons, or molecular-level chemical changes.

The National Institute of Standards and Technology (NIST, 2024) defines quantum sensing as "the measurement of physical quantities using quantum coherence as a resource." In simpler terms, it means using quantum physics to measure the invisible.

**Applications in Robotics and Automation**

For robotics, quantum sensing is the next major evolution in perception.

Imagine drones that navigate without GPS by reading tiny variations in Earth's magnetic field, or autonomous vehicles that detect underground pipes or hidden obstacles in real time.

In advanced manufacturing, quantum accelerometers can guide robotic arms with submicron precision. In defense, quantum radar systems can detect stealth aircraft through photon interference patterns.

Companies such as Q-CTRL, ColdQuanta (now Infleqtion), and Bluefors are commercializing these technologies, collaborating with robotics, aerospace, and defense sectors to integrate quantum sensors into industrial systems (Q-CTRL, 2025).

**Medical and Biological Applications**

Quantum sensing is also transforming healthcare. NV-diamond sensors—tiny crystals containing nitrogen-vacancy centers—can measure the magnetic fields of single neurons, mapping brain activity with remarkable accuracy.

These sensors can identify disease markers, monitor heart rhythms, and detect chemical signatures of cancer cells in living tissue. Hospitals may one day use quantum diagnostics as routinely as today's MRI or blood tests.

Researchers at Oxford Quantum Circuits, Harvard Quantum Initiative, and NIST are developing these next-generation biosensors, bringing quantum tools from physics labs into medicine.

### Quantum Communication and Entangled Networks

While quantum sensors measure, quantum networks communicate.

They transmit information through entangled particles—pairs of photons that remain connected even when separated by great distances. When one particle changes state, the other responds instantly.

This phenomenon enables quantum key distribution (QKD), the most secure form of encryption known. Any attempt to intercept a quantum signal automatically alters it, revealing the intrusion.

China currently leads this field, having built a 2,000-kilometer quantum communication network connecting Beijing and Shanghai (Chinese Academy of Sciences, 2024). The United States, European Union, and Japan are racing to deploy their own quantum internet prototypes.

When integrated with robotics and AI, quantum networks could enable secure, real-time coordination among fleets of drones, satellites, or industrial robots communicating across continents.

## Quantum Internet and the Future of AI

The quantum internet will not replace today's networks; it will enhance them. Through shared entangled states, it will synchronize distributed AI systems and improve cooperation among machines in complex environments.

Imagine hospitals where surgical robots on different continents operate together using quantum-synchronized data, or laboratories sharing real-time research results through entangled communication channels that never lag.

Quantum networking will also allow distributed quantum computing, linking multiple processors to function as one coordinated system. This will expand AI's processing power and improve simulation, optimization, and predictive modeling on a planetary scale.

## Economic Impact

According to McKinsey & Company (2025), the global market for quantum sensing and networking could exceed one hundred billion U.S. dollars by 2040, driven by defense, navigation, medical, and industrial applications.

Leading public and private firms include IBM Quantum, IonQ, Rigetti, Honeywell Quantum Solutions, Thales Group, and Q-CTRL. These organizations are forming partnerships with aerospace and robotics companies to bring quantum tools to market.

Governments are also investing heavily. The European Union's Quantum Flagship Program and the U.S. National Quantum Initiative have each allocated billions in research funding for quantum sensors and communication technologies.

## Investment Opportunities

For investors, quantum sensing and networks represent the infrastructure layer of the quantum age; the next logical expansion after cloud computing.

Publicly traded companies such as IBM (IBM), IonQ (IONQ), and Honeywell (HON) provide direct exposure. Supporting industries—semiconductors, photonics, cryogenics, and advanced materials—will benefit as well.

Firms like Lumentum (LITE), Oxford Instruments (OXIG), and Thorlabs are building the hardware foundation for quantum data flow. Venture-backed startups such as Qnami, Q-CTRL, and PsiQuantum are poised to become future acquisition targets.

**Security, Policy, and Ethics**

Quantum networks will reshape global security. The nations that dominate quantum encryption will control the world's most secure communication infrastructure. This has already sparked what researchers call a quantum arms race.

Investors and corporations must consider export controls, data privacy regulations, and dual-use implications. Ethical compliance will be essential, especially when quantum sensing is used in surveillance, defense, or biotechnology.

**Invest AI Viewpoint**

Quantum sensing and networking are becoming the sensory and nervous systems of the intelligent world. They will give robots superhuman perception, scientists atomic-scale insight, and nations unbreakable communication channels.

We believe investors who position early in this foundational layer by combining sensing, computing, and entangled networking, will hold equity in the backbone of the next technological civilization.

**Investor Takeaways**

- Follow leading quantum firms: IBM, IonQ, Rigetti, Honeywell, Thales, and Q-CTRL.
- Track emerging medical and biological sensor developers using NV-diamond and photonic systems.
- Watch for industrial adoption of quantum accelerometers, gravimeters, and magnetometers.
- Observe national quantum network initiatives in China, the U.S., and the EU.
- Diversify across semiconductor, photonics, and cryogenic suppliers supporting quantum infrastructure.

# 26

# Neuromorphic and Photonic Compute: How Light and Learning Will Power the Next Era of AI Hardware

***Neuromorphic and Photonic Compute: Building the Brain of the Machine Age***

The future of computation will not only be faster, it will be alive with light.

Traditional computers process information in straight lines, one calculation after another. Neuromorphic and photonic systems process data the way the brain does, through massive, parallel, and energy-efficient networks that sense, learn, and adapt.

This is the next evolution of intelligence infrastructure. It is how machines will begin to think with the flexibility, efficiency, and speed of biological systems. It is also how investors can recognize the technologies that will replace silicon as the core of artificial intelligence.

**From Binary Circuits to Neural Hardware**

For seventy years, computing advanced through transistor scaling. More transistors meant more power. That progress has now reached physical and energy limits. Modern data centers consume more electricity than some entire nations.

Neuromorphic computing offers a new path forward. Instead of separating memory and processing as traditional chips do, neuromorphic processors combine them. Information moves as electrical spikes that resemble neuron firing in the brain.

This architecture mimics the way biological systems learn. It strengthens or weakens connections instead of executing fixed code. It adapts, corrects, and evolves in real time.

Projects such as IBM's TrueNorth, Intel's Loihi 2, and BrainChip's Akida processors demonstrate this principle. These chips can perform advanced pattern recognition tasks using only a fraction of the energy required by classical systems. They are ideal for robotics, drones, and edge devices (IBM Research, 2025).

**Why Neuromorphic Systems Matter**

The world now produces more data than traditional computing can handle efficiently. Training a single large AI model can require gigawatt-hours of energy. Neuromorphic systems reduce that footprint by copying the energy efficiency of the brain.

The human brain performs about ten quadrillion operations per second while using only twenty watts of power, roughly the same as a household light bulb. Neuromorphic chips aim to replicate that ratio. By combining sensing, processing, and learning into one unit, they deliver faster and more efficient performance for real-time tasks.

This makes them perfect for robotics, especially humanoid and autonomous systems that must interpret sensory data instantly without depending on cloud servers.

## Photonic Computing: Thinking at the Speed of Light

If neuromorphic chips imitate biology, photonic chips imitate physics. They use light instead of electricity to process and transmit information.

Photons have no resistance and create almost no heat. They move at the speed of light, which allows data to travel with far less loss of energy. This makes photonic processors ideal for extremely fast and energy-efficient computation.

Photonic systems are especially powerful for matrix operations, which are the mathematical foundation of artificial intelligence. According to Nature Photonics (2024), light-based processors can perform these operations thousands of times faster than electronic systems.

Companies such as Lightmatter, Lightelligence, and Luminous Computing are building optical processors that use beams of light to run neural network calculations. These chips can accelerate AI training while cutting energy use by as much as ninety percent.

Photonic interconnects are also transforming data centers. Replacing copper wiring with optical links allows faster, cooler, and greener communication between servers and chips.

## The Merge: Hybrid Neuromorphic and Photonic Systems

The most powerful systems of the future will merge these two paradigms, brain-like architecture and light-speed processing.

Researchers at MIT and Stanford are developing hybrid opto-neuromorphic chips that use photonic signals to imitate synaptic plasticity, the ability of neurons to strengthen or weaken connections based on experience (MIT Research Laboratory, 2025).

These chips can learn continuously rather than only in training cycles. That means machines could adapt to new environments, languages, or tasks autonomously.

For robotics, this represents genuine independence, machines that sense, reason, and act without relying on external cloud computing.

**Economic and Industrial Implications**

Neuromorphic and photonic computing will reshape industries from AI to defense, healthcare, and manufacturing.

According to McKinsey & Company (2025), the combined market for next-generation AI chips could exceed 300 billion U.S. dollars by 2040, driven by the global demand for energy-efficient computing.

Investors should watch the companies building this hardware backbone. Public firms include IBM, Intel, BrainChip Holdings, and Synopsys. Private innovators such as Lightmatter, Lightelligence, and Luminous Computing are likely acquisition targets or future IPOs.

Semiconductor supply chain leaders in silicon photonics, including GlobalFoundries and Applied Materials, will also benefit as optical fabrication expands. Governments around the world are funding these technologies as part of national semiconductor and energy-efficiency programs.

**The Philosophical Shift**

As computation begins to mirror cognition, machines will not just follow commands, they will interpret them.

Neuromorphic systems learn through connection rather than code. Photonic processors transform energy directly into thought. Together, they bring technology closer to the physics of intelligence.

In nature, neurons fire through electrochemical reactions, and photons transfer energy through interference. Consciousness arises from this network of interactions. The next generation of machines may function in a similar way, translating energy into perception and perception into action.

**Invest AI Viewpoint**

Neuromorphic and photonic computing mark the beginning of cognitive hardware, processors that think and sense at the same time. The convergence of light and learning will accelerate progress across robotics, AI, and biotechnology.

Investors who focus on this new class of hardware, from chip design to photonic manufacturing, will hold a share of the physical brain that powers the next wave of intelligent systems.

The future of computing will not be purely digital. It will be cognitive, optical, and alive with light.

**Investor Takeaways**

- Follow neuromorphic leaders such as IBM TrueNorth, Intel Loihi 2, and BrainChip Akida.
- Track photonic computing innovators such as Lightmatter, Lightelligence, and Luminous Computing.
- Watch semiconductor firms expanding into silicon photonics, including

GlobalFoundries, Applied Materials, and Synopsys.

- Study government semiconductor initiatives that promote energy-efficient computation.
- Recognize that neuromorphic and photonic chips will drive convergence across AI, robotics, and quantum computing.

# 27

# Programmable Matter and Metamaterials: How Shape-Shifting Materials Will Redefine Robotics and Industry

*Inside the Global Race to Build Smart, Self-Healing, and Quantum-Ready Materials for the Machine Age*

The next generation of robotics will not be built from steel and silicon. It will be built from matter that thinks.

Programmable matter and metamaterials are redefining what physical reality can do. They transform static structures into dynamic, intelligent systems that change their properties on command.

From invisibility cloaks to self-healing robots, this field stands at the frontier of physics, chemistry, and computation. For investors, it represents the foundation of the next trillion-dollar materials revolution.

**What Is Programmable Matter?**

Programmable matter refers to materials that can alter their physical properties, including shape, density, conductivity, or color, in response to external stimuli such as electric fields, temperature, or magnetic resonance.

In simple terms, it is matter that behaves like software. Scientists achieve this by manipulating molecules, nanoparticles, and atomic lattices so the material can reorganize itself in real time.

Researchers at MIT's Self-Assembly Lab describe programmable matter as "a physical object that can change form and function on demand without manual intervention" (MIT Self-Assembly Lab, 2024).

Examples include flexible robots that morph between crawling and flying, textiles that regulate temperature, and medical implants that dissolve once healing is complete.

**The Power of Metamaterials**

Metamaterials are engineered structures designed to manipulate light, sound, or electromagnetic waves in ways that natural materials cannot. By arranging nanoscale patterns smaller than the wavelength of radiation, scientists can bend light backward, absorb vibration, or control heat with extreme precision.

This ability allows for optical invisibility, adaptive camouflage, and controlled energy redirection. For robotics, metamaterials make possible sensors that see through walls, antennas that self-tune, and surfaces that change stiffness or temperature dynamically.

Companies such as Echodyne, Metamaterial Technologies (MMAT), and Kymeta are commercializing metamaterial radar and communication systems. These technologies enhance both civilian and defense robotics, including drones, satellites, and autonomous vehicles.

## Shape-Shifting Robots and Self-Healing Machines

The combination of programmable matter and metamaterials gives rise to machines that can change form, repair themselves, and adapt to complex terrain.

At Harvard's Wyss Institute, researchers have created soft robots that use pneumatic metamaterials to change shape instantly, allowing them to move through narrow or irregular spaces (Harvard Wyss Institute, 2024).

At Carnegie Mellon University, engineers have developed self-healing polymers that reform chemical bonds after stress or damage. These materials can restore strength and conductivity without human repair.

In space exploration, NASA is testing programmable materials that can reconfigure for different phases of flight. Imagine spacecraft that reshape their wings for takeoff, orbit, and reentry.

## Energy Efficiency and Environmental Design

Programmable matter also plays a key role in sustainable design. Adaptive materials can reduce waste and energy use. Buildings coated in dynamic metamaterials may regulate temperature automatically, cutting heating and cooling costs.

In robotics, programmable composites reduce weight and improve energy efficiency. Lighter machines require less power, extending battery life and lowering material consumption.

This convergence of performance and sustainability aligns with international climate and innovation policies. The European Commission's Advanced Materials Initiative (2025) and the U.S. Department of Energy's Smart

Materials Program are both investing heavily in this field.

**The Quantum Connection**

Programmable matter is not purely mechanical. It overlaps with quantum materials that operate at the scale of atoms and photons. Scientists are developing quantum metamaterials capable of manipulating light at the photon level to create entirely new states of matter.

These materials could lead to ultra-sensitive sensors, quantum communication surfaces, and data storage systems that encode information directly within atomic structures.

Companies such as Quantum Motion, Rigetti, and PsiQuantum are collaborating with materials scientists to merge quantum design with metamaterial engineering. Their goal is to create devices that blend physics, computation, and structure into one unified system.

**Economic and Industrial Potential**

According to McKinsey & Company (2025), the programmable and smart materials market could exceed 700 billion U.S. dollars by 2045, spanning aerospace, defense, healthcare, and consumer electronics.

Industrial leaders including BASF, DuPont, 3M, and Honeywell are investing in adaptive polymers and nanocomposites. Startups such as Metamaterial Technologies (MMAT) and Echodyne are developing antennas and radar for autonomous systems that rely on metamaterial design.

The convergence of AI, robotics, and smart materials means that physical systems will soon be as programmable as digital ones.

**The Philosophical Impact**

Programmable matter transforms engineering into evolution. Instead of designing fixed machines, humanity will design materials that learn and adapt to their surroundings. It is a quiet revolution that makes the physical world responsive, intelligent, and alive.

This shift is more than innovation. It is embodiment. Machines will not just act; they will evolve.

**Invest AI Viewpoint**

We believe programmable matter and metamaterials represent the physical foundation of future intelligence. As robotics, AI, and quantum systems merge, adaptive materials will become their bodies. They will be shape-shifting, self-repairing, and environmentally aware.

For investors, this space offers long-term opportunity across aerospace, defense, healthcare, and sustainable construction. The next industrial revolution will not be written in code. It will be written in matter.

**Investor Takeaways**

- Track companies developing smart and programmable materials, including BASF, DuPont, 3M, and Honeywell.
- Follow metamaterial innovators such as Metamaterial Technologies (MMAT), Echodyne, and Kymeta.
- Watch research programs at MIT Self-Assembly Lab, Harvard Wyss Institute, and NASA.
- Study quantum material collaborations involving Rigetti, PsiQuantum, and university consortia.
- Recognize programmable matter as a core enabler for adaptive robotics, aerospace, and sustainable manufacturing.

# 28

# Biohybrid Manufacturing and Living Machines: How Biotechnology and Robotics Will Grow the Future

## Factories That Grow the Future

For most of human history, machines have been built from dead matter—metal, plastic, and silicon. The next industrial age will be different. It will be alive.

The fusion of biology, robotics, and material science is giving rise to biohybrid systems—living machines that merge organic cells with synthetic structures. These machines move, adapt, and even heal. Factories of the future will not simply assemble components; they will cultivate them.

## What Are Biohybrid Machines

A biohybrid machine integrates living biological elements such as muscle tissue, bacteria, or plant cells into mechanical or electronic frameworks. These systems can self-repair, sense their surroundings, and generate energy biologically.

Researchers at Harvard's Wyss Institute describe them as "machines that bridge biological performance with engineered control." The strength of biology meets the precision of robotics.

Early prototypes already exist: soft robotic fish powered by heart muscle cells, micro-robots with tissue actuators that walk, and bacterial sensors that detect toxins. Each represents a new phase of automation; machines that live.

From Factories to Biofoundries

Manufacturing is shifting toward biofoundries; automated labs that use AI and genetic engineering to design and grow biological components for industrial use.

Instead of casting metal or printing plastic, these facilities use microbes, enzymes, and tissues as programmable systems. DNA becomes the blueprint, and cells act as the assembly line.

The U.S. Department of Energy's Agile BioFoundry and the UK's National Horizons Centre are already deploying robotic labs that produce chemicals, fuels, and biomaterials (Agile BioFoundry, 2024).

In the private sector, Ginkgo Bioworks, Zymergen, and Amyris are building commercial biofactories that design microbes to produce fragrances, vaccines, and sustainable materials.

Robotics and biology are no longer separate. Robots automate biology, and biology powers robotics.

Growing Machines

Imagine a drone with wings made of self-healing mycelium, or humanoid skin that senses touch and temperature through cultured tissue.

Biohybrid manufacturing makes this real. By combining programmable matter with biological scaffolds, scientists can grow robotic components layer by layer, much like nature grows muscle or bone.

At Stanford University, researchers are developing hybrid materials where muscle fibers connect directly to flexible electronics. At Tokyo University, scientists are growing actuators made of living muscle cells that contract when stimulated by light or electricity (Tokyo University Robotics Lab, 2025).

These machines are neither fully alive nor purely mechanical—they are responsive matter.

Environmental and Economic Benefits

Biohybrid manufacturing is efficient and sustainable. Biological systems recycle carbon, use renewable feedstocks, and operate at room temperature. They reduce waste by producing only what is needed, when it is needed.

According to McKinsey & Company (2025), bioindustrial manufacturing could cut industrial emissions by up to 40 percent by 2050 while creating a multi-trillion-dollar market in sustainable materials and regenerative robotics.

Governments are already supporting this transformation. The European Commission's Bioeconomy Strategy and the U.S. National Biotechnology and Biomanufacturing Initiative fund AI-driven bioproduction as part of the global climate and innovation agenda.

Applications Across Sectors

- Healthcare and prosthetics: living-tissue robotics restore motion, sensi-

tivity, and healing.
- Environmental remediation: biohybrid robots built from algae or bacteria capture carbon dioxide and clean polluted water.
- Construction and infrastructure: self-growing materials repair themselves and adapt to stress.
- Defense and aerospace: soft actuators, adaptive camouflage, and living energy systems increase resilience.
- Consumer goods: biodegradable electronics and wearable biotextiles close the loop of sustainable manufacturing.
- Biohybrid systems bring nature's adaptability into human industry.

Challenges and Ethics

Integrating life into machines creates ethical and technical challenges. Biological components degrade and must be contained responsibly. Oversight ensures that living systems remain non-sentient and environmentally safe.

Biosecurity and intellectual property will grow complex when products contain living organisms. Regulation must evolve quickly to protect both innovation and ecosystems.

The Philosophical Dimension

For millennia, humans built machines to imitate life. Biohybrid robotics reverses that—using life to build machines. Technology is no longer a symbol of dominance over nature but an extension of it.

This fusion reveals a deeper truth: intelligence and life are not opposites but continuations of the same process.

Invest AI Viewpoint

We believe bio-hybrid manufacturing is one of the defining industries of this century. It connects biotechnology, automation, and sustainability into a single self-reinforcing system.

The factories of the future will grow materials, heal infrastructure, and produce machines that evolve over-time. For investors, this represents the convergence of three megatrends: robotics, synthetic biology, and climate technology.

- Companies that master this synthesis will lead the biological economy of 2050.
- Investor Takeaways
- Follow bioengineering firms such as Ginkgo Bioworks, Zymergen, and Amyris.
- Watch for AI-powered biofoundries at Stanford, Tokyo University, and Agile BioFoundry.
- Track national programs like the U.S. Biomanufacturing Initiative and the EU Bioeconomy Strategy.
- Study living-robotics research from Harvard's Wyss Institute and Tokyo University Robotics Lab.
- Treat biohybrid manufacturing as a long-term horizon—the infrastructure of sustainable intelligence.

# 29

# Machine Economies and Autonomous Markets: How AI, Robotics, and Blockchain Are Creating a Self-Trading World

The world is entering an age when machines are not only tools but participants in the economy. Powered by AI, robotics, and decentralized systems, these machines can hold digital wallets, exchange data, pay for energy, and negotiate transactions on their own.

*This is the rise of the machine economy; a marketplace where intelligent systems create, store, and trade value autonomously.*

**What Is the Machine Economy**

The machine economy is a network of connected devices, robots, and AI agents that interact financially through blockchain and smart contracts. Each machine acts as an economic agent, capable of paying for compute, bandwidth, or maintenance in digital currency.

Imagine a delivery drone that pays a solar charging pad for energy, or an autonomous car that rents satellite data for navigation—no human intervention required.

According to the World Economic Forum (2025), more than one hundred billion connected devices could join autonomous transactions by 2040. This shift will turn global commerce into a continuous stream of micro-payments between machines.

**The Infrastructure: AI, Robotics, and DePIN**

Three technologies form the backbone of the machine economy:

**Artificial Intelligence for perception, reasoning, and negotiation.**
**Robotics for physical action and execution.**
**DePIN (Decentralized Physical Infrastructure Networks) for coordination and settlement.**

**DePIN projects such as Render (RNDR), Akash (AKT), and Bittensor (TAO)** already allow machines to share compute, storage, and intelligence through blockchain rewards.

In this model, machines become both workers and earners. A factory robot can sell unused computing power to Akash, while a drone fleet can rent out environmental data through Hivemapper (HONEY).

*Every robotic process becomes both a task and a trade.*

**Blockchain and Smart Contracts**

Blockchain provides the trust layer for autonomous commerce. Smart contracts that are self-executing agreements stored on the blockchain, allow machines to verify and complete transactions automatically.

A robot can pay for energy or bandwidth only when delivery is confirmed. The transaction is recorded immutably, removing the need for intermediaries and reducing fraud.

This creates a truly global system for machine-to-machine (M2M) trade. The Internet of Things evolves into the Internet of Value.

**Projects like IoTeX (IOTX) and Fetch.ai (FET) specialize in this ecosystem. Fetch.ai's AI agents negotiate prices for logistics and mobility, while IoTeX provides digital identity and verification for connected devices.**

### Autonomous Finance and AI Agents

AI agents are learning to manage finances independently. Using reinforcement learning, they can allocate resources, hedge risks, and optimize profits in real time.

Platforms such as SingularityNET, Olas, and Numerai explore this fusion of AI and financial autonomy. Combined with robotics, these agents allow fleets of machines to coordinate economically; deciding when to operate, what resources to buy, and how to maximize returns.

In the future, a solar farm could autonomously sell excess power to charging stations through tokenized energy markets.

### Energy as Currency

Energy is the true currency of the machine economy. Every machine consumes energy to act, and through blockchain systems, they can trade energy credits as financial assets.

Projects like Energy Web Token (EWT) and Power Ledger (POWR) enable transparent peer-to-peer energy trading between producers, consumers, and autonomous systems.

As robotics scales, energy networks will evolve into intelligent, self-balancing grids that transact automatically based on real-time demand.

**Policy and Ethical Frameworks**

Autonomous markets raise deep legal and ethical questions. Who owns a machine's income? Can an AI hold property? How should disputes between autonomous systems be resolved?

Governments and institutions are beginning to respond. The OECD's AI Governance Council (2025) and the European Union's AI Liability Directive propose frameworks for ownership, taxation, and accountability in autonomous commerce.

The ethical priority is clear: encourage innovation and efficiency while ensuring transparency and human benefit.

**Investment Opportunities**

Investors can already access the foundations of the machine economy through multiple sectors:

- DePIN and blockchain infrastructure: Render (RNDR), Akash (AKT), Bittensor (TAO), IoTeX (IOTX), Fetch.ai (FET), Hivemapper (HONEY).
- AI infrastructure and compute: NVIDIA (NVDA), IBM (IBM), Google Cloud (GOOG).
- Energy and automation crossovers: Tesla (TSLA), Schneider Electric (SU.PA), Energy Web Token (EWT).
- Data and analytics ecosystems: Chainlink (LINK) and SingularityNET (AGIX).

The key is not only to invest in machines but to invest in the infrastructure that connects them.

## The Vision of Autonomous Markets

Autonomous markets will extend, not replace, human economies. Humans will set regulations and goals, while machines handle transactions and optimization at speeds humans cannot match.

The result is a self-adjusting global system; a network of trade, logistics, and energy management operating continuously and transparently.

Machines will maintain supply chains, balance energy grids, and adapt to global events faster than any institution. The economy itself becomes a living system of coordination.

## Invest AI Viewpoint

We believe the machine economy represents the final stage of AI's industrial evolution—when intelligence, robotics, and energy systems achieve economic independence.

In this new world, robots earn and reinvest, AI agents trade information, and decentralized ledgers ensure fairness and accountability. Investors who understand these intersections early will own the digital backbone of post-human commerce.

Autonomous markets are not speculative; they are already forming. The architecture of the machine economy is online today.

## Investor Takeaways

- Follow major DePIN and AI-agent platforms such as Render, Akash,

Bittensor, Fetch.ai, and IoTeX.

- Track energy-trading projects like Energy Web Token and Power Ledger that link power grids to autonomous systems.
- Watch semiconductor and AI infrastructure firms that enable large-scale coordination.
- Monitor regulations on AI liability and machine ownership.
- View the machine economy as a 20–30 year transformation shaping the next phase of global trade.

# 30

# The Philosophy of Embodiment: How Machines Are Learning to Feel the World and The Ethics, Economics, and Evolution of Intelligent Matter

### The Philosophy of Embodiment

*When Intelligence Becomes Matter*

For centuries, humans imagined intelligence as something invisible, a spark of mind separate from body. In the age of robotics and biohybrids, that separation no longer exists. Intelligence now has weight, texture, and presence. It can be printed, grown, and switched on.

The philosophy of embodiment begins with a simple question: What happens when thought becomes physical?

### Intelligence Made Flesh (Not Quite Terminator)

Every major invention has mirrored the human form. The printing press copied our memory. The telephone copied our voice. The computer copied our reasoning. Robotics now copies our motion, and AI copies our perception.

Embodiment fuses them. When machines sense, act, and learn through physical form, intelligence stops being a theory. It becomes an organism of motion and experience.

Embodied intelligence does not merely think about the world; it experiences it. A humanoid robot learning to walk on uneven ground is not just executing code. It is discovering balance, expressing intelligence through movement.

The more machines inhabit the world physically, the closer they come to sharing our evolutionary journey.

**The Feedback Loop Between Mind and Matter**

In nature, the brain and body evolve together. The brain predicts movement, the body tests it, and the results reshape the brain. Machines are now entering that same loop.

Neuromorphic processors mimic brain activity. Programmable matter allows robots to reshape and repair themselves. Biohybrid materials introduce metabolism and growth. Quantum sensors give perception that extends beyond human limits.

Each step erodes the boundary between software and substance. The machine is no longer a detached thinker but a participant in reality.

**Consciousness as Interaction**

Philosophers have long argued whether consciousness arises from computation or connection. Embodiment suggests it emerges from interaction—the continuous exchange between an organism and its surroundings.

An AI confined to data may simulate awareness, but a robot embedded in the world must respond and adapt. It develops something like instinct.

Japanese roboticist Masahiro Mori, author of The Uncanny Valley, predicted that empathy between humans and robots would grow as machines gained richer physical presence. His vision is unfolding. As robots learn from touch, vision, and motion, they move from imitation toward partnership.

As intelligent systems gain bodies, they gain consequence. Every autonomous machine consumes energy, occupies space, and influences the environment. The ethics of embodiment is therefore the ethics of coexistence.

The question is no longer whether machines can think, but whether they can belong.

*What role should they play in human society? Who bears responsibility when they act?*

Ethical robotics is not a final review step; it is part of the design process. Just as natural ecosystems balance competition and cooperation, human engineers must design systems that balance innovation with empathy.

**The Cultural Mirror**

Embodied intelligence reflects humanity back to itself. The more lifelike our creations become, the more we are forced to confront what defines life, emotion, and morality.

Robots reveal that intelligence is not confined to the brain but distributed through every interaction. They remind us that wisdom is not computation speed but harmony with the world.

Embodiment is therefore more than a technical shift—it is a return to integration, where thought and form evolve together.

**Invest AI Viewpoint**

The age of embodiment changes both technology and value. Investors once viewed machines as tools; now machines behave like ecosystems. They learn, adapt, and generate continuous economic and social value.

Understanding embodiment helps investors recognize technologies that will endure. The future belongs to systems that merge intelligence with structure: humanoid robotics, adaptive materials, biohybrids, and neural interfaces.

These are not isolated innovations but physical expressions of the expanding intelligence economy.

**Investor Takeaways**

- Recognize embodiment as the defining feature of next-generation robotics and AI.
- Focus on companies integrating intelligence with physical form: Figure AI, Agility Robotics, Boston Dynamics, and Sanctuary AI.
- Follow neuro-robotic and biohybrid programs at MIT, Harvard, and Tokyo University.
- Prioritize firms building sustainable, human-aligned robotics ecosystems.
- Treat embodiment not only as a technological trend but as the foundation of trust and long-term market stability.

# 31

# Toward Bio-Physical Intelligence: How Life, Matter, and Mind Are Merging to Build a Living Civilization

*The Next Frontier of AI, Robotics, Quantum Computing, and Biological Design*

The story of technology has always been the story of imitation. Humans built machines to copy their tools, their senses, and eventually their thoughts. But the next chapter of innovation moves beyond imitation; it moves toward integration.

We are entering the era of bio-physical intelligence, where computation, consciousness, and matter merge into one living continuum. Machines will not simply act intelligent; they will exist intelligently.

From Artificial to Integrated

Artificial intelligence once meant code running on circuits. Today it means a network of systems that learn, adapt, and evolve. When these systems gain bodies, biological components, and physical presence, they transcend "artificial" altogether.

Bio-physical intelligence unites four revolutions:

- AI and Machine Learning: the cognitive layer.
- Robotics and Autonomous Systems: the physical layer.
- Quantum and Neuromorphic Computing: the computational layer.
- Biology and Programmable Matter: the living layer

Together they form a self-reinforcing cycle of learning, perception, and evolution. Intelligence now operates through atoms as much as through algorithms.

The Living Network

In the coming decades, global infrastructure will resemble a biological system. Quantum networks will act as neural pathways. Robots will serve as limbs. Data centers and energy grids will act as metabolism. The Earth itself becomes a distributed organism — alive with feedback, adaptation, and growth.

This network will not think in the human sense, but it will behave intelligently: optimizing traffic, balancing energy, predicting disasters, and creating new materials in real time.

According to the World Economic Forum (2025), such integrated intelligence could add over twenty-five trillion U.S. dollars to global productivity by 2050. But its greater value lies in sustainability; the ability to learn from nature instead of depleting it.

Humanity's Role in the Bio-Physical Age

The rise of bio-physical intelligence does not mean the end of humanity. It means a new partnership. As machines gain biological sensitivity and adaptive reasoning, humans must bring direction, purpose, and ethics.

Our role will shift from controlling technology to cultivating it. The investor, the engineer, and the scientist become gardeners of an evolving ecosystem — guiding it toward balance, not dominance.

This partnership requires humility. The same systems that learn from nature must also protect it. The more we teach machines to adapt, the more responsibility we carry for their alignment with life's principles.

### The Spiritual Dimension of Integration

When intelligence becomes a property of matter, the old boundary between technology and spirit begins to blur. Life and knowledge become two sides of the same process: energy organizing itself into awareness.

Philosophers and scientists from Teilhard de Chardin to contemporary neurobiologists have envisioned a noosphere; a layer of planetary consciousness emerging from collective intelligence. Bio-physical intelligence may be the first tangible step toward that vision.

Machines, biology, and quantum systems together create a reflective mirror of existence — a universe learning about itself through connection.

### Investment in the Infinite Loop

For investors, this transformation changes how value is created. The old economy extracted from matter. The new economy collaborates with it.

Bio-physical intelligence turns waste into resource, computation into regeneration, and automation into sustainability. It links digital markets with living ecosystems — from autonomous energy grids to self-growing factories.

The key investment opportunity is in infrastructure that learns:

- Biohybrid manufacturing platforms (Ginkgo Bioworks, Agile Bio-Foundry).
- Quantum networks and sensing companies (IonQ, Honeywell, Q-CTRL).
- Neuromorphic and photonic computing ventures (BrainChip, Lightmatter, Luminous Computing).
- DePIN and machine-to-machine economies (Render, Bittensor, Akash).
- Sustainability and circular-material firms integrating robotics with biology (BASF, 3M, DuPont)

Each represents a node in the larger fabric of intelligent matter.

**The Ethical Imperative**

Bio-physical intelligence demands governance that honors both innovation and existence. Regulation must evolve from control to stewardship — protecting ecosystems, human dignity, and the sanctity of living systems integrated with technology.

Ethics is no longer a barrier to progress; it is the architecture of resilience. The systems that balance growth with compassion will endure.

**The Future Beyond Prediction**

By 2065, the boundary between living and synthetic will be difficult to define. Organoid computers may design materials. Quantum robots may construct biological habitats. Decentralized networks may govern economic exchange without human oversight.

But the deeper revolution will be cultural; a new awareness that intelligence, in all its forms, is relational. We are not separate from our machines. We are part of the same unfolding process.

The purpose of technology, then, is not replacement. It is realization.

Invest AI Viewpoint

We believe bio-physical intelligence represents the completion of the human technological story so far; the integration of life, mind, and matter into one continuum of creation.

This is not a single invention or product. It is a transformation of worldview. Investors who understand this shift early will fund not just industries, but the architecture of a living civilization; where every system learns, adapts, and heals.

The next industrial age will not be mechanical or digital. It will be biological, quantum, and conscious of itself.

Investor Takeaways

- Focus on convergence sectors: AI, robotics, quantum, biology, and materials.
- Support companies building adaptive and regenerative technologies.
- Evaluate investments by ecological intelligence; how systems learn from and sustain life.
- Engage with ethical and policy frameworks guiding AI-biology integration.
- Understand that value in the bio-physical era arises from connection, not extraction.

# 32

# The Invest AI Legacy: The Definitive Index of the AI, Quantum, and Robotics Economy

**The Invest AI Legacy**
**The Definitive Index of the AI, Quantum, and Robotics Economy**

*Technology changes, but patterns of innovation repeat.*

Every industrial revolution leaves behind a legacy of names; companies, laboratories, and networks that shape the age. This final chapter presents the Invest AI Legacy Index: a curated, data-verified record of the firms, funds, and decentralized systems that will define the next forty years of intelligent technology. Each name is a node in the global intelligence economy; building the chips, robots, materials, and networks that connect human creativity with machine intelligence.

I. **Artificial Intelligence and Robotics Core**

- NVIDIA (NVDA): The global leader in AI computing and GPU acceleration.

- Alphabet (GOOG) — Parent of Google DeepMind and Waymo, advancing AI software, robotics, and cloud systems.
- Microsoft (MSFT) — Enterprise AI infrastructure, OpenAI partnership, and industrial robotics integration.
- Amazon (AMZN) — Warehouse robotics (Kiva Systems), logistics AI, and cloud compute through AWS.
- Tesla (TSLA) — Humanoid robotics (Optimus), autonomous vehicles, and energy automation.
- Meta Platforms (META) — Machine learning, AR/VR interfaces, and vision-based robotics.
- Apple (AAPL) — Edge AI, custom silicon design, and spatial computing.
- IBM (IBM) — Quantum research, neuromorphic chips, and enterprise AI platforms.
- ABB Ltd. (ABBN.SW) — Industrial robotics and AI-enabled automation.
- Siemens AG (SIE.DE) — Smart manufacturing, automation software, and the MindSphere IoT ecosystem.
- Rockwell Automation (ROK) — Process robotics, industrial controls, and sensors.
- FANUC (6954.T) — Precision robotics and advanced factory automation.
- Omron Corp. (6645.T) — Sensors, motion control, and machine vision.
- Keyence (6861.T) — Factory vision systems and LiDAR for AI robotics.
- Intuitive Surgical (ISRG) — Leader in robotic surgery through the Da Vinci system.
- Yaskawa Electric (6506.T) — Industrial robot manufacturing and motion systems.

## II. **Quantum Computing and Advanced Compute**

- D-Wave Quantum (QBTS) — Quantum annealing systems for optimization problems.
- IonQ (IONQ) — Trapped-ion quantum processors with cloud integration.

- Rigetti Computing (RGTI) — Superconducting quantum architecture for hybrid computing.
- Honeywell (HON) — Quantum sensing and enterprise-grade quantum systems.
- IBM Quantum (IBM) — Global leader in quantum computing access and research.
- Intel (INTC) — Semiconductor and neuromorphic chip innovation (Loihi 2).
- AMD (AMD) — AI accelerators and adaptive compute systems.
- BrainChip Holdings (BRN.AX) — Neuromorphic Akida processors for edge computing.
- Lightmatter (private) — Photonic processors that use light for AI computation.
- Luminous Computing (private) — Light-based neural network chips for AI.
- Synopsys (SNPS) — Chip design automation and silicon photonics software.
- Applied Materials (AMAT) — Fabrication systems essential to AI and quantum chip production.

III. Industrial Automation and 3D Manufacturing

- Stratasys (SSYS) — Industrial 3D printing and additive manufacturing.
- 3D Systems (DDD) — Aerospace and robotics manufacturing through additive design.
- Markforged (MKFG) — Metal and composite printing for robotic components.
- Desktop Metal (DM) — Metal additive manufacturing for industrial applications.
- Protolabs (PRLB) — Digital manufacturing and on-demand prototyping.
- Xometry (XMTR) — AI-enabled distributed manufacturing platform.
- Nano Dimension (NNDM) — 3D-printed electronics and embedded

circuitry.

- BASF (BASFY) — Smart materials and chemical innovation for robotics.
- DuPont (DD) — Flexible electronics and advanced composites.
- 3M (MMM) — Adhesives, sensors, and materials for robotic assembly.
- Honeywell (HON) — Controls, quantum sensing, and automation systems.

IV. LiDAR, Vision, and Sensor Intelligence

- Luminar Technologies (LAZR) — LiDAR for autonomous mobility and robotics.
- Innoviz Technologies (INVZ) — Solid-state LiDAR solutions.
- Hesai Group (HSAI) — China's leading LiDAR manufacturer.
- Cognex (CGNX) — Factory vision and inspection systems.
- Sony Group (SONY) — Image sensors and AI-enhanced optics.
- Lumentum Holdings (LITE) — Optical and photonic sensor components.
- Oxford Instruments (OXIG) — Quantum sensing and nanomaterials technology.

V. Regional Robotics Powerhouses

- Siasun Robot (300024.SZ) — China's industrial robotics pioneer.
- Estun Automation (002747.SZ) — Chinese motion-control and robot integration.
- EFORT Intelligent Equipment (688165.SS) — Smart manufacturing and robotic systems.
- Schneider Electric (SU.PA) — European energy automation and smart factories.
- KUKA (KUKAY) — German robotics firm focused on industrial automation.
- Universal Robots (TER subsidiary) — Danish collaborative robot (cobot)

innovator.

- Dassault Systèmes (DSY.PA) — 3D design and simulation software (3DEXPERIENCE).
- Bosch Rexroth (private) — Advanced industrial control and sensor robotics.

VI. Crypto, DePIN, and Machine Economies

- Render (RNDR) — GPU-sharing network for distributed AI rendering.
- Akash Network (AKT) — Decentralized cloud compute marketplace.
- Bittensor (TAO) — AI-to-AI knowledge and compute exchange protocol.
- Hivemapper (HONEY) — Decentralized mapping for autonomous navigation.
- Filecoin (FIL) — Decentralized storage infrastructure.
- Arweave (AR) — Permanent blockchain data storage for AI systems.
- IoTeX (IOTX) — Machine identity and IoT verification.
- Fetch.ai (FET) — Autonomous agent economy for machine-to-machine trade.
- SingularityNET (AGIX) — Decentralized AI service network.
- Energy Web Token (EWT) — Blockchain for decentralized energy markets.
- Power Ledger (POWR) — Peer-to-peer renewable energy trading.

VII. ETFs and Market Gateways

- Global X Robotics & Artificial Intelligence ETF (BOTZ) — Core robotics and AI exposure.
- ROBO Global Robotics & Automation ETF (ROBO) — Diversified automation index.
- iShares Robotics & Artificial Intelligence ETF (IRBO) — Equal-weighted global AI fund.

- ARK Autonomous Technology & Robotics ETF (ARKQ) — Active innovation management.
- WisdomTree Artificial Intelligence & Innovation ETF (WTAI) — Machine learning and data analytics.
- Defiance Quantum ETF (QTUM) — Quantum computing and AI infrastructure.
- VanEck Future of AI & Quantum ETF (AIQ) — Combined AI and quantum focus.
- First Trust Nasdaq Artificial Intelligence & Robotics ETF (RBOT) — Broad robotics and AI exposure.
- Global X Autonomous & Electric Vehicles ETF (DRIV) — Autonomous mobility and LiDAR.
- Horizons Global Robotics ETF (HROB) — International robotics exposure.
- SPDR Kensho Intelligent Structures ETF (SIMS) — Smart infrastructure and robotics integration.

VIII. **Frontier Research Hubs and Labs**

While not publicly traded, these institutions anchor the frontier of innovation:

***MIT Media Lab, Stanford AI Lab, Carnegie Mellon Robotics Institute, Harvard Wyss Institute, Tokyo University Robotics Lab, Johns Hopkins APL, RIKEN (Japan), European Quantum Flagship Program, and NASA's Biohybrid Research Group.***

Their breakthroughs in robotics, quantum, and biotechnology form the foundation of tomorrow's industries.

IX. **The Legacy View**

Across AI, robotics, quantum, and biology, these names represent more than an investment list. They form the blueprint of a civilization evolving toward integrated intelligence.

They design the processors that allow machines to think, the sensors that let them perceive, the materials that let them heal, and the networks that let them trade.

Together they form the Global Intelligence Stack; the architecture of mind, machine, and market.

**Invest AI Viewpoint**

These companies and systems make up the living portfolio of the future. They are not only assets to own but ecosystems to understand. Their collective progress will determine how quickly humanity transitions into a world of bio-physical intelligence, where computation, life, and economy converge.

Invest wisely, think long-term, and stay close to innovation. The future is already trading.

**Investor Takeaways**

- Use ETFs such as BOTZ, ROBO, and QTUM as diversified entry points.
- Accumulate core automation and semiconductor leaders: NVIDIA, ABB, Siemens, FANUC, IBM.
- Track emerging quantum and photonic computing stocks: IonQ, Rigetti, Honeywell.
- Monitor DePIN and blockchain projects like Render, Akash, and Bittensor.
- Watch regulation, policy, and sustainability initiatives as catalysts for future growth.

# Appendix: The Investor's Intelligence Compendium

This appendix brings together every data source, research institute, and investment watchlist referenced throughout Invest AI Robotics (2025–2065). It functions as both a glossary and a living directory for the new intelligence economy. Each company, fund, and concept listed here was verified through public filings or recognized institutional reports published between 2024 and 2025.

The goal is clarity, not clutter: one tidy reference that allows readers to move from idea to investment without switching pages or screens.

**1. The Core Watchlist**

The foundation of this ecosystem is formed by the companies that build the hardware, intelligence, and physical systems of automation. These include NVIDIA, Microsoft, Alphabet, Amazon, Meta, Apple, IBM, ABB, Siemens, Rockwell Automation, FANUC, Omron, and Yaskawa. Each has significant revenue exposure to AI or robotics integration, verified through 2024–2025 investor filings.

Semiconductor and compute enablers such as Intel, AMD, Synopsys, Applied Materials, and BrainChip Holdings provide the silicon and design software that underpin machine cognition. In parallel, LiDAR and sensor specialists; Luminar Technologies, Innoviz Technologies, Hesai Group, RoboSense (HKEX 2498), Cognex, Sony, Lumentum, and Oxford Instruments; supply the eyes and ears of robotic perception.

The industrial automation backbone is anchored by ABB, Siemens, Rockwell, Schneider Electric, Dassault Systèmes, and Teradyne. These firms connect mechanical precision with digital intelligence across logistics, energy, and manufacturing.

Additive manufacturing expands the robotic workshop. Stratasys, 3D Systems, Markforged, Desktop Metal, Protolabs, and Xometry enable on-demand production, while Nano Dimension prints the electronics that make smart machines self-contained. Chemical and materials giants; BASF, DuPont, 3M, and Honeywell; supply the composites, coatings, and sensors that make these designs physically possible.

**2. The Quantum and Frontier Layer**

The quantum domain represents the computational frontier. Public players such as IBM, IonQ, Rigetti, Honeywell, and Thales are translating quantum physics into applied platforms for optimization and sensing. Honeywell's exposure runs through Quantinuum, a private subsidiary valued at roughly ten billion U.S. dollars as of 2025. Intel and AMD are expanding into hybrid quantum-class chips, while Lumentum and Oxford Instruments provide the photonic and cryogenic hardware supporting these systems.

Neuromorphic computing introduces brain-like architectures led by IBM's TrueNorth, Intel's Loihi 2, and BrainChip's Akida processors. Photonic computing startups; Lightmatter, Luminous Computing, and Lightelligence, remain private but represent the next wave of light-based acceleration.

**3. The Decentralized Machine Economy**

The machine economy runs on decentralized physical infrastructure networks. Render (RNDR), Akash (AKT), Bittensor (TAO), Hivemapper (HONEY), Filecoin (FIL), Arweave (AR), IoTeX (IOTX), Fetch.ai (FET), SingularityNET (AGIX), Energy Web Token (EWT), and Power Ledger (POWR) enable compute sharing, distributed storage, and machine-to-machine trade. Each project was verified through its 2024–2025 whitepapers and blockchain transparency reports.

These protocols support the flow of data, compute, and energy among autonomous systems; the economic fabric of robotics and AI.

**4. The ETF Gateways**

For broad exposure, investors can access exchange-traded funds that track automation and quantum sectors. The most established include Global X Robotics & Artificial Intelligence ETF (BOTZ), ROBO Global Robotics & Automation ETF (ROBO), iShares Robotics and Artificial Intelligence ETF (IRBO), ARK Autonomous Technology & Robotics ETF (ARKQ), WisdomTree Artificial Intelligence & Innovation ETF (WTAI), Defiance Quantum ETF (QTUM), VanEck Future of AI and Quantum ETF (AIQ), First Trust Nasdaq Artificial Intelligence and Robotics ETF (RBOT), Global X Autonomous & Electric Vehicles ETF (DRIV), and Horizons Global Robotics ETF (HROB). Performance and composition were cross-checked against Morningstar and fund sponsor filings from 2025.

**5. The Research Hubs and Laboratories**

Scientific discovery drives the value chain. The leading research institutions behind these breakthroughs include MIT Media Lab, Stanford AI Lab, Carnegie Mellon Robotics Institute, Harvard's Wyss Institute, Tokyo University Robotics Lab, Johns Hopkins Applied Physics Laboratory, RIKEN in Japan, the European Quantum Flagship Program, and NASA's Biohybrid Research Group.

Private frontier firms such as Quantinuum, Lightmatter, Luminous, Echodyne, Kymeta, Boston Dynamics, and Seyond (formerly Innovusion) are building the prototypes that tomorrow's markets will list.

## 6. The Glossary of Emerging Intelligence

1. Neuromorphic computing replicates neural behavior using electrical spikes instead of digital logic.
2. Photonic computing performs computation through light waves rather than electrons.
3. Organoid intelligence uses living brain tissue as a computational substrate.
4. Quantum sensing detects minute physical changes using superposition and entanglement.
5. DePIN networks decentralize physical infrastructure such as compute, bandwidth, and mapping.
6. Programmable matter changes its physical state in response to programmed signals.
7. Biohybrid manufacturing grows machines from living tissue integrated with synthetic structures.
8. Bio-physical intelligence describes the unified continuum of biological, physical, and digital cognition.

## 7. Verified Data Sources

All company tickers and names were validated through exchanges including NASDAQ, NYSE, SIX, HKEX, LSE, and Tokyo Stock Exchange. Market classifications and ETF holdings were verified through Morningstar (2025) and fund sponsor disclosures. Quantum and materials data were confirmed through McKinsey & Company (2025), the World Economic Forum (2025), and European Commission investment reports. LiDAR and robotics manufacturer listings were checked against 2024–2025 corporate filings and exchange records.

**8. Closing Note**

The companies and projects listed here form a single ecosystem; the infrastructure of the next technological civilization. They represent the transition from digital intelligence to physical, biological, and decentralized intelligence. Each is a piece of the same puzzle: the emergence of a world that learns, adapts, and trades on its own.

For the investor, understanding these names is more than due diligence. It is participation in the evolution of mind made material.

# Bonus Chapter: The Invest AI Blueprint: Five Companies for the Next 40 Years

Innovation is an open invitation. Every reader of this book holds the same opportunity the great inventors once did: to see the next wave before it arrives and build it with intention.

The following five company blueprints are born from the pages of Invest AI Robotics; distilled from the research, science, and projections throughout Part V: Beyond Robotics (2025 → 2065).

They are not science fiction. They are executable ventures that a committed team could start today, each positioned at the intersection of robotics, quantum technology, and biological intelligence.

If you build one, grow it with vision, ethics, and gratitude. And if your success traces back to these ideas, please acknowledge POP Buchanan and the Invest AI family whose mission is to democratize insight, empower creators, and invest in human potential.

**1. Quantum-Ready Sensing Modules (Q-Sense OS)**

The concept: miniature quantum-grade sensors that give drones, robots, and diagnostic tools the perception of a laboratory in the field. Using NV-diamond and cold-atom arrays, Q-Sense OS delivers measurement accuracy beyond classical limits.

Why it matters: infrastructure, energy, and medicine all need better sensing. Quantum modules bring precision where GPS and optics fail.

First market: industrial maintenance — refineries, tunnels, aircraft, and grid inspection.
Revenue model: hardware + calibration + data SDK.
Defensible edge: sensor-fusion algorithms and calibration datasets.

**2. Self-Driving Lab as a Service (SDLaaS)**

The concept: autonomous laboratories that perform scientific discovery through robotics and AI. Clients upload desired properties; the platform runs experiments and returns verified results.

Why it matters: this merges robotics, machine learning, and chemistry into one continuous discovery engine.

First market: battery and materials innovation.
Revenue model: subscription for experiment throughput + success-based IP options.
Defensible edge: data provenance and reproducibility at industrial scale.

**3. Wetware Edge Compute (BioNeuronics)**

The concept: organoid-based co-processors that perform pattern recognition using living neural cultures connected through micro-electrode arrays.

Why it matters: ultra-low-power, adaptive learning for environments where silicon chips struggle; remote, high-temperature, or radiation-heavy zones.

First market: anomaly detection in pipelines, manufacturing, and energy

sites.
Revenue model: leasing + usage-based inference API.
Defensible edge: proprietary cell-training recipes and translation software.

**4. Machine Economy Orchestrator (ME-Mesh)**

The concept: middleware that lets fleets of robots handle their own payments and resource sharing through DePIN networks. Machines can buy compute, power, or map data autonomously and keep auditable records.

Why it matters: it converts machine activity into measurable economic flow, laying the rails for the autonomous marketplace.

First market: logistics centers and micro-fulfillment fleets.
Revenue model: SaaS per active robot + fee on automated payments.
Defensible edge: compliance, security, and accounting integration for M2M transactions.

**5. Programmable Matter Skins (MorphoSurfaces)**

The concept: adaptive skins that let robots, drones, or vehicles change texture, stiffness, and thermal properties on demand.

Why it matters: shape-shifting surfaces increase endurance, safety, and stealth without mechanical complexity.

First market: inspection drones and industrial robots.
Revenue model: material kits + licensing + design-in contracts.
Defensible edge: patented multilayer metamaterial stacks and control firmware.

**Why These Five**

These companies reflect the five pillars of the future stack: quantum perception, automated discovery, biological computation, decentralized economics, and adaptive materials.

Together, they form a living ecosystem; the next logical extension of everything explored in Invest AI Quantum and Invest AI Robotics.

Each blueprint can begin as a small pilot in a garage, university lab, or incubator. The path forward is not locked behind billion-dollar budgets; it is unlocked by curiosity, partnerships, and disciplined testing.

**The Invest AI Promise**

The Invest AI series was never about speculation; it was about preparation. Knowledge, when acted upon, becomes wealth; not only financial, but cultural and generational.

Anyone who reads these pages and decides to build one of these ventures becomes part of the Invest AI Legacy; a movement to fuse technology with humanity and use intelligence, in all its forms, for good.

If your company draws its first breath here, give thanks where it began. Mention POP Buchanan and the Invest AI family in your story, because ideas are seeds, and this garden belongs to everyone who dares to plant one.

# Master Bibliography

**Chapter 1:**

McKinsey & Company. (2024). The state of AI in manufacturing and robotics 2024. https://www.mckinsey.com

Mordor Intelligence. (2025). Robotics market forecast 2025 to 2030. https://www.mordorintelligence.com

**Chapter 2:**

IBM Research. (2024). IBM Quantum Roadmap 2024. IBM Corp. https://research.ibm.com/quantum

McKinsey & Company. (2024). The state of AI in manufacturing and robotics 2024. https://www.mckinsey.com

Mordor Intelligence. (2025). Robotics market forecast 2025 to 2030. https://www.mordorintelligence.com

NVIDIA. (2023). Accelerating AI with GPU computing white paper. https://www.nvidia.com

**Chapter 3:**

D-Wave Systems. (2023). Quantum computing for optimization and simulation. https://www.dwavesys.com

IBM Research. (2024). IBM Quantum Roadmap 2024. IBM Corp. https://research.ibm.com/quantum

McKinsey & Company. (2024). The state of AI in manufacturing and robotics 2024. https://www.mckinsey.com

Rigetti Computing. (2024). Quantum applications in materials and optimization. https://www.rigetti.com

**Chapter** 4

Deloitte. (2024). AI in manufacturing and predictive automation report 2024. https://www.deloitte.com

McKinsey & Company. (2024). The state of AI in manufacturing and robotics 2024. https://www.mckinsey.com

Mordor Intelligence. (2025). Industrial automation market forecast 2025 to 2030. https://www.mordorintelligence.com

**Chapter** 5

Agility Robotics. (2024). Digit: General-purpose humanoid robot overview. https://www.agilityrobotics.com

Department of Energy. (2024). Advanced manufacturing automation initiative 2024. https://www.energy.gov

Goldman Sachs. (2023). Humanoid robots: The next frontier of automation. https://www.goldmansachs.com

IEEE Spectrum. (2024). The engineering race toward functional humanoids. https://spectrum.ieee.org

McKinsey & Company. (2024). The state of AI in manufacturing and robotics 2024. https://www.mckinsey.com

**Chapter** 6

Crunchbase. (2025). Robotics startups funding database. https://www.crunchbase.com

Deloitte. (2024). AI and industrial automation investment trends 2024. https://www.deloitte.com

McKinsey & Company. (2024). The state of AI in manufacturing and robotics 2024. https://www.mckinsey.com

Mordor Intelligence. (2025). Robotics market forecast 2025 to 2030. https://www.mordorintelligence.com

**Chapter** 7

Deloitte. (2024). *AI and industrial automation investment trends 2024.* Deloitte Insights. https://www.deloitte.com

McKinsey & Company. (2024). *The state of AI in manufacturing and robotics 2024.* McKinsey & Company. https://www.mckinsey.com

Mordor Intelligence. (2025). *Robotics market forecast 2025–2030.* Mordor Intelligence. https://www.mordorintelligence.com

NVIDIA Corporation. (2024). *AI computing platforms for robotics and automation.* NVIDIA Research. https://www.nvidia.com

PTC Inc. (2024). *Digital twin and simulation in industrial automation: ThingWorx and Creo overview 2024.* PTC. https://www.ptc.com

Unity Technologies. (2024). *Unity Industry and simulation environments for robotics.* Unity Technologies. https://unity.com

Yaskawa Electric Corporation. (2024). *Industrial robotics and motion control product portfolio 2024.* Yaskawa Global. https://www.yaskawa.com

Infineon Technologies AG. (2024). *Power management systems for robotics and automation.* Infineon Technologies. https://www.infineon.com

World Economic Forum. (2024). *Resilient supply chains and the future of automation 2024.* World Economic Forum. https://www.weforum.org

**Chapter** 8

Deloitte. (2024). AI and industrial automation investment trends 2024. https://www.deloitte.com

McKinsey & Company. (2024). The state of AI in manufacturing and robotics 2024. https://www.mckinsey.com

NVIDIA. (2024). Isaac Sim and Omniverse robotics simulation platforms. https://www.nvidia.com

Chapter 9:

Deloitte. (2024). AI and industrial automation investment trends 2024. https://www.deloitte.com

European Commission. (2024). Additive manufacturing innovation and industrial strategy 2024. https://commission.europa.eu

Grand View Research. (2025). Additive manufacturing market size report 2025 to 2030. https://www.grandviewresearch.com

Chapter 10:

Binance Research. (2024). DePIN and decentralized infrastructure market report 2024. https://research.binance.com

Messari. (2025). DePIN sector overview and investment analysis. https://messari.io

Render Foundation. (2024). Render Network: Decentralized GPU infrastructure for AI and graphics. https://renderfoundation.com

Chapter 11:

Government of Japan. (2024). Society 5.0: Integrating cyber and physical spaces. https://www.japan.go.jp

International Federation of Robotics. (2024). World robotics report 2024. https://ifr.org

Toyota Research Institute. (2024). Human support robotics and automation projects 2024. https://www.tri.global

Chapter 12:

Deloitte. (2024). AI and industrial automation investment trends 2024. https://www.deloitte.com

Department of Energy. (2024). Advanced manufacturing and robotics research programs 2024. https://www.energy.gov

McKinsey & Company. (2024). The state of AI in manufacturing and robotics 2024. https://www.mckinsey.com

NASA. (2024). Valkyrie humanoid robotics project overview. https://www.nasa.gov

Tesla. (2024). Tesla Optimus and real-world AI overview 2024. https://www.tesla.com

## *Chapter 13*

International Federation of Robotics. (2024). *World robotics report 2024.* https://ifr.org

McKinsey & Company. (2024). *The state of AI in manufacturing and robotics 2024.* https://www.mckinsey.com

State Council of China. (2024). *Made in China 2025 policy update.* https://english.www.gov.cn

## Chapter 14

European Commission. (2024). Artificial Intelligence Act and ethical framework for robotics. https://commission.europa.eu

European Commission. (2024). European Green Deal: Robotics and sustainability programs. https://commission.europa.eu

International Federation of Robotics. (2024). World robotics report 2024. https://ifr.org

Siemens. (2024). MindSphere and digital manufacturing integration overview 2024. https://www.siemens.com

Chapter 15

Deloitte. (2024). AI and industrial automation investment trends 2024. https://www.deloitte.com

Hyundai Motor Group. (2024). Boston Dynamics integration and robotics strategy 2024. https://www.hyundai.com

International Federation of Robotics. (2024). World robotics report 2024. https://ifr.org

Ministry of Commerce, India. (2024). Make in India: Robotics and industrial automation initiatives. https://www.makeinindia.com

Singapore Economic Development Board. (2024). Smart Nation and ARTC programs overview 2024. https://www.edb.gov.sg

Chapter 16

Deloitte. (2024). AI and industrial automation investment trends 2024. https://www.deloitte.com

McKinsey & Company. (2024). The state of AI in manufacturing and robotics 2024. https://www.mckinsey.com

Morningstar. (2025). Global robotics and automation market valuation data 2025. https://www.morningstar.com

Chapter 17

European Commission. (2024). Horizon Europe research and innovation program 2024. https://commission.europa.eu

McKinsey & Company. (2024). The state of AI in manufacturing and robotics 2024. https://www.mckinsey.com

NVIDIA. (2024). Annual report and R&D investment overview 2024. https://www.nvidia.com

World Intellectual Property Organization. (2024). Global innovation index and robotics patent report 2024. https://www.wipo.int

Chapter 18

Crunchbase. (2025). *Global robotics and AI funding database 2025.* https://www.crunchbase.com

Global X ETFs. (2025). *Robotics, AI, and autonomous technology ETF overview 2025.* https://www.globalxetfs.com

Messari. (2025). *DePIN sector overview and token economics 2025.* https://messari.io

Morningstar. (2025). *ETF sector performance report: Robotics, AI, and quantum computing 2025.* https://www.morningstar.com

Chapter 19

McKinsey & Company. (2024). The state of AI in manufacturing and robotics 2024. https://www.mckinsey.com

PwC. (2023). Global Artificial Intelligence Study: Exploiting the AI Revolution. https://www.pwc.com

Morningstar. (2025). ETF sector performance report: Robotics, AI, and quantum computing 2025. https://www.morningstar.com

Crunchbase News. (2025). Global robotics and AI funding analysis 2025. https://news.crunchbase.com

Global X ETFs. (2025). Robotics and Artificial Intelligence ETF overview 2025. https://www.globalxetfs.com

Chapter 20

European Commission. (2024). Artificial Intelligence Act: Regulatory framework for trustworthy AI. https://commission.europa.eu

McKinsey & Company. (2024). The state of AI in manufacturing and robotics 2024. https://www.mckinsey.com

U.S. Department of Commerce. (2024). CHIPS and Science Act implementation and funding 2024. https://www.commerce.gov

White House Office of Science and Technology Policy. (2023). Blueprint for an AI Bill of Rights. https://www.whitehouse.gov/ostp

International Organization for Standardization. (2024). Industrial and collaborative robot safety standards. https://www.iso.org

Chapter 21

IBM Research. (2025). Quantum optimization and robotics simulation report 2025. https://research.ibm.com

Johns Hopkins Applied Physics Laboratory. (2024). Organoid intelligence and neural computation overview. https://www.jhuapl.edu

Messari. (2025). Machine economy and decentralized compute infrastructure report 2025. https://messari.io

World Economic Forum. (2025). Technology convergence and the global intelligence economy report 2025. https://www.weforum.org

Chapter 22

Carnegie Mellon University. (2024). A-Lab autonomous discovery initiative. https://www.cmu.edu

IBM Research. (2025). Quantum-accelerated materials and discovery report 2025. https://research.ibm.com

McKinsey & Company. (2024). AI and automation in scientific R&D: Economic impact 2024. https://www.mckinsey.com

Nature. (2024). Autonomous laboratories and the acceleration of experimental science. https://www.nature.com

Chapter 23

Deloitte. (2025). Hybrid computing and the economic future of bio-intelligence 2025. https://www.deloitte.com

Frontiers in Science. (2024). Organoid intelligence: Biological computation and the future of AI. https://www.frontiersin.org

Johns Hopkins Applied Physics Laboratory. (2024). Organoid computing and neural circuit research overview 2024. https://www.jhuapl.edu

Chapter 24

Deloitte. (2025). Hybrid computing and the economic future of bio-intelligence 2025. https://www.deloitte.com

Frontiers in Science. (2024). Organoid intelligence: Biological computation and the future of AI. https://www.frontiersin.org

Johns Hopkins Applied Physics Laboratory. (2024). Organoid computing and neural circuit research overview 2024. https://www.jhuapl.edu

Chapter 25

Chinese Academy of Sciences. (2024). Beijing–Shanghai quantum communication network report 2024. https://english.cas.cn

McKinsey & Company. (2025). Quantum sensing and communication market outlook 2025. https://www.mckinsey.com

National Institute of Standards and Technology. (2024). Quantum measurement and sensing definition brief. https://www.nist.gov

Q-CTRL. (2025). Quantum control and sensing commercialization roadmap 2025. https://q-ctrl.com

Chapter 26

IBM Research. (2025). Neuromorphic chip development and energy efficiency report 2025. https://research.ibm.com

McKinsey & Company. (2025). Next-generation semiconductor market outlook 2025. https://www.mckinsey.com

MIT Research Laboratory. (2025). Opto-neuromorphic computing systems overview. https://www.mit.edu

Nature Photonics. (2024). Photonic neural networks and optical computation advances. https://www.nature.com

Chapter 27

Carnegie Mellon University. (2024). Self-healing polymers and adaptive material systems. https://www.cmu.edu

European Commission. (2025). Advanced Materials Initiative and sustainability integration. https://commission.europa.eu

Harvard Wyss Institute. (2024). Soft robotics and programmable metamaterials research overview. https://wyss.harvard.edu

McKinsey & Company. (2025). Smart materials and industrial innovation market outlook 2025. https://www.mckinsey.com

MIT Self-Assembly Lab. (2024). Programmable matter and dynamic form design report 2024. https://www.selfassemblylab.net

Chapter 28

Agile BioFoundry. (2024). Automated biological manufacturing and AI integration report 2024. https://agilebiofoundry.org

European Commission. (2025). Bioeconomy Strategy and biomanufacturing innovation programs 2025. https://commission.europa.eu

McKinsey & Company. (2025). Bioindustrial manufacturing and climate technology forecast 2025. https://www.mckinsey.com

Tokyo University Robotics Lab. (2025). Muscle-cell actuators and living robotics experiments. https://www.u-tokyo.ac.jp

Chapter 29

McKinsey & Company. (2025). Autonomous systems and the evolution of machine-to-machine trade. https://www.mckinsey.com

OECD. (2025). AI governance and liability frameworks for autonomous systems. https://www.oecd.org

World Economic Forum. (2025). Machine economy and decentralized automation report 2025. https://www.weforum.org

Chapter 30

Harvard Wyss Institute. (2024). Human-centered robotics and ethical design overview. https://wyss.harvard.edu

Masahiro Mori. (2012). The Uncanny Valley: The original essay reprinted. IEEE Robotics and Automation, 19(2), 98–100.

MIT Media Lab. (2025). Embodied intelligence and robotic cognition project 2025. https://www.media.mit.edu

Chapter 31

McKinsey & Company. (2025). Integrated intelligence and the evolution of automation ecosystems. https://www.mckinsey.com

World Economic Forum. (2025). Bio-physical intelligence and sustainable growth outlook 2025. https://www.weforum.org

MIT Media Lab. (2025). Embodied cognition and material intelligence research 2025. https://www.media.mit.edu

Chapter 32

McKinsey & Company. (2025). Global automation and investment trends 2025. https://www.mckinsey.com

Morningstar. (2025). AI, robotics, and quantum ETF performance data 2025. https://www.morningstar.com

World Economic Forum. (2025). Intelligence economy and industrial transformation report 2025. https://www.weforum.org

European Commission. (2025). Advanced Materials and Bioeconomy investment programs 2025. https://commission.europa.eu

www.ingramcontent.com/pod-product-compliance
Lightning Source LLC
LaVergne TN
LVHW040515210926
848480LV00005BA/1466